DEVIANT JOURNALISM FROM THE LOST GENERATION

JESSE AIZENSTAT

Published by:
Casbah Publishing
P.O. Box 5173
Santa Barbara, CA 93150
Casbahpublishing@gmail.com
www.bloggingthecasbah.com

Printed in Canada

Publisher's Cataloging-in-Publication data

Aizenstat, Jesse.
Surfing the Middle East / Jesse Aizenstat.
p. cm.
ISBN 9780983700913
1. Aizenstat, Jesse. 2. Surfing --Biography. 3. Middle East--Guidebooks. 4. Surfing --Middle East --Guidebooks. 5. Surfing --Israel --Guidebooks. 6. Surfing --Lebanon --Guidebooks. 7. Middle East--Politics and government--21st century. I. Title.

GV840.S8 .A39 2011
797.3/2 --dc22   2011914088

Cover designed by *the*BookDesigners | www.bookdesigners.com
Insert designed by Zack Suhadolnik | www.zacksdesigns.com
Produced by Brookes Nohlgren | www.booksbybrookes.com
Edited by Donna Beech | www.donnabeech.com

This book is dedicated to the werewolf in us all.

The edge is still Out there.

HUNTER S. THOMPSON

ACKNOWLEDGMENTS

Let me first express my gratitude to the people of the Eastern Mediterranean. Though I briefly met many of you, it was your overall hospitality and friendship that carried me through this adventure. Special thanks to Lee Jordan, the Haifa surfers, and Monner Moukaddem, to name a few.

Much credit also goes to the talented team at Zentro Media and Digital Ranch for turning *Surfing the Middle East* into an incredibly cool iPad app. To producer Jim Lindsay for his unwavering encouragement. And to Shiva Media for making an iPhone app that's just that cool.

To the wonderful people I had the pleasure to work with at Casbah Publishing: Brookes Nohlgren, Dr. James Gelvin, Graham Van Dixhorn, Lisa McCann, Vicky Ondracek, Blake Bronstad, Zack Suhadolnik, Julien Bassan, and *the*BookDesigners. To those who helped turn the early manuscript into a book: Michael Taft, Steven Kotler, Reza Aslan, George Hale, Amanda Jones, and Thom Lynch. And to the dearest of friends, Marilee Zdenek: may the late afternoon continue to bloom.

To the highly skilled Donna Beech: friend, editor, "spiritual advisor," and the first non-genetically related person who believed that a book should be attempted.

To my brother, Eli, and sister, Alia. And to my loving parents, Stephen Aizenstat and Maren Hansen. Without your care and support, I'd still be changing your oil at the gas station.

I am grateful.

MAPS

CONTENTS

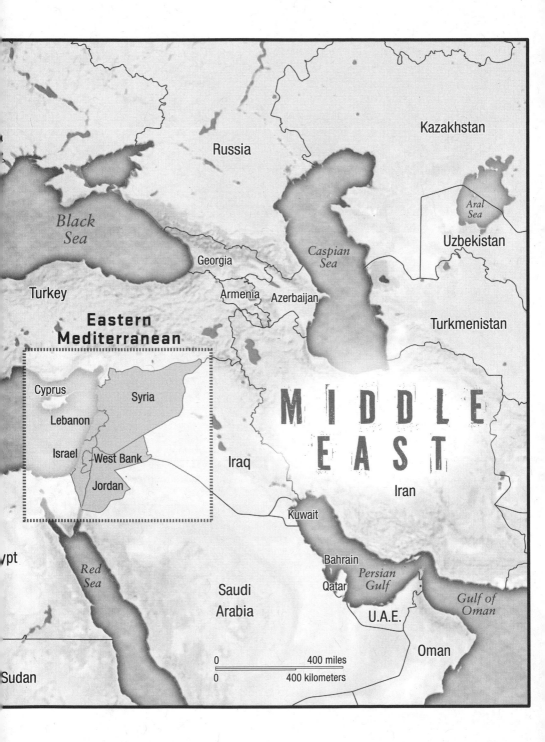

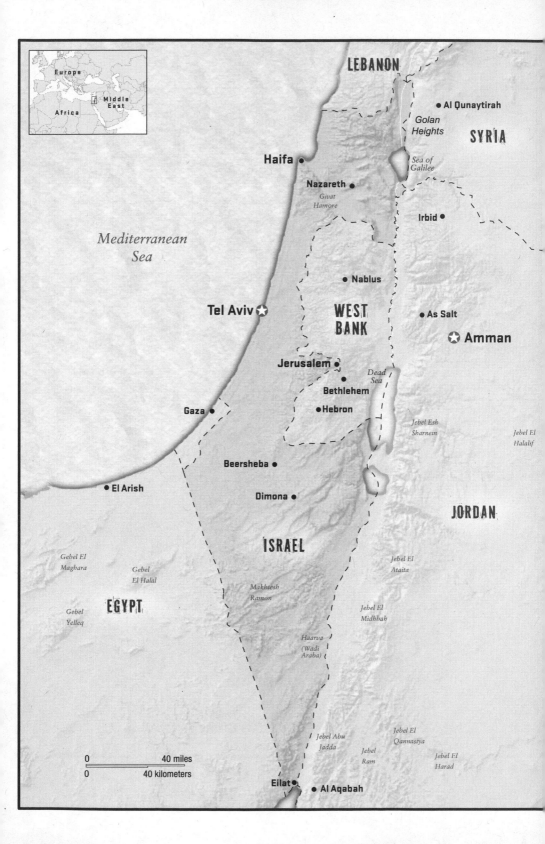

PREFACE

Until this deviant little adventure, surfing and the Middle East existed on different continents for me. They represented two parts of myself that my California buddies said simply could not go together. And sweet blue-eyed Jesus, can you blame them? Combining my two most unlikely passions took more than creative chutzpah. Like scoring good waves, it took conditions.

When I graduated from college in May 2009, the U.S. job market was in the worst shape since the Great Depression. By every measure it seemed that our parents' generation had blown it so badly with the American housing crisis that all hopes for entering the middle class were now being chased with crude sour mash. And lots of it.

With my own options dwindling, I received a letter in the mail saying that I had narrowly flunked the grammar section of the Foreign Service Exam. My backup plan was to hop aboard a foreign non-governmental organization, but that idea was ended by unforeseen budget cuts. Most of my fellow graduates were either swallowing their pride and moving back in with their parents or settling for some job that was unrelated to their increasingly irrelevant bachelor of arts degree. As for the lucky few who found something career oriented, most were underemployed, transplanted to some funky town no one had ever heard of, and perhaps most grave, taken from the magical shores of the Pacific Ocean. None of this had much allure to me. But it helped create an environment where surfing the Middle East as a journalist seemed like a good idea.

Second to the American job economy, the other reason I embarked on this adventure was the cold hard fact that for most of my schooling life I'd been dismissed as a hopeless dumbass. From a very young age I was fond of learning about the world but grew restless in the classroom and wanted to go out to experience the world myself. Dyslexia and my struggles in school were a mixture of jangled thoughts and emotional whippings . . . and yet, the difficulty I faced made it easier to question the rules of the so-called objective game. I learned to become responsible for myself and fight twice as hard as the people around me to pass through the same green light. A teacher once said to me, "Disability is always blessed with opportunity." And by the time I got to college, I believed that my blunderings in school had cultivated a different kind of thinking that was going to help me in ways I had yet to understand.

And so it was on just an ordinary day, meandering along the Pacific Coast Highway looking for surf, that the actual idea of surfing from Israel to Lebanon came to me. I knew that nobody had ever done it before. And I felt a sort of strange comfort knowing the Israeli-Lebanese border was closed. Figuring out how to get around "closed things" called upon the same practical skills I developed as a child with learning disabilities.

With only months before graduation, I wrote seemingly endless emails to magazine editors, trying to find someone to support my unique surf-journalist endeavor. But nobody wanted the story. Editors either ignored me or assumed that (1) I couldn't deliver the story, (2) I didn't have the background, or (3) I couldn't surf the Middle East. Eventually, the *Surfer's Journal* showed interest. They weren't going to pay much and they didn't do advances. They gave me the famous editorial line, "Send us what you've got when you've got it." Of course, this would be after the fact, with no guarantees.

My next challenge would be dealing with the reality of crossing the Israeli-Lebanese border. It is closed—with all sides armed, fortified, and constantly striking matches to test the combustibility of the place. Getting everyone along the Eastern Mediterranean to lay down their arms for a lone California surfer to "explore the coast" and "tell a journalistic story" would be out of the question. So, I would have to "go around" . . . meaning that after I found surf in northern Israel, I would have to go back, down through Jerusalem, across the West Bank, to the inland airport in Jordan, and then fly over Syria to an airport in Beirut that would not be welcoming to my travels.

I would need a second American passport. Lebanon is still officially at war with Israel, and anyone with an Israeli stamp is automatically denied entry. I knew it wasn't going to be easy—or even achievable—but I had heard rumors of war correspondents taking the inland route from Israel to Lebanon before. Just not with a surfboard.

So, I thought, *what the hell?* I didn't have a job. I had just skipped my college graduation ceremony to go to a bullfight in Tijuana. I had nothing to lose. And so a few days later I left for the Middle East on a fully subsidized Birthright Israel trip, on a mission to surf the last place anyone expected: the Middle East. A wild adventure and my first job out of college: to tell the story of surfing from Israel to Lebanon, around a most menacing, war-torn border.

Making my way up to Haifa, Israel, with my bag and my surfboard, Che

FIRST LEG

"IT'S LIKE MAUI WITH ROCKETS"

All my life my heart has sought a thing I cannot name.

REMEMBERED LINE FROM
A LONG-FORGOTTEN POEM

CUS IMA SHELHA!!!

*Curiosity, earnest research to learn the hidden laws of
nature, gladness akin to rapture, as they were unfolded
to me, are among the earliest sensations I can remember.*

MARY SHELLEY, *Frankenstein*

"Cus ima shelha!" yelled the Israeli cab driver. *Cus ima shelha* is one
of those insults *all* Israeli cab drivers hold at the ready—it literally
means "your mother's cunt."

I yelled back in English. "Hey, dude, look! The surfboard
goes better in the front seat when the back is down!" But the
dense bastard didn't listen. He hadn't a clue what this long,
flat object was or that it could even break. All he knew was
crude physics: a surfboard shoved is a surfboard fit. And like
a maniac, he kept wildly rearranging Che in the tiny trunk of
his junky jalopy.

"Goddammit!" I shrieked. *"Shukran! Shukran!"* ("Thank
you! Thank you!") I firmly grabbed my board from the persistent
jerk's hands. The sun was high and I was in no mood for this. I
was back—in the Haifa paradise I remembered.

With Che in hand, I rushed to the next waiting cabbie and
dropped a quick "Shalom!" I hoped he would honor a common
decency among Jews and allow *me* to load Che into the taxi myself.
He did, but probably not because I mustered a tacky "shalom."

Whatever the reason, I was grateful. Che was my only
friend along the Israeli coast and I didn't schlep him all the
way from North America to see him get smashed by some
hot-blooded cabbie. Minus the tie, this dude was dressed in a

decent suit that had all the right creases in all the right places and a pair of well-worn black leather shoes. He was old and had that traditional/respectable thing going for him, and he looked like he was truly from that mythic, Eastern European place my Jewish grandfather talked about . . . the Old Country.

Gingerly, I lowered his front seat and placed Che on top of its firm cushion. I climbed into the back with my bag. The gentle old man fired up his engine. We were off. When it works, traveling with a surfboard can be that easy.

———

As the cab glided over the freshly paved highway to the Port Inn, I remembered the place fondly. Haifa is truly a refuge from the religion of Jerusalem and the booze of Tel Aviv.

And sweet Jesus! The Port Inn! Two years earlier, in 2007, on my last trip along the Eastern Mediterranean, I would sit on the plant-filled balcony, my eyes wandering over the swerving, canyon-like roads that casually meandered into the ancient casbah—the remnants of historic Palestine . . . and even times before then. In the afternoons, in this seaside haven, I'd stroll the fringes of the Old City. From the vacant south, there's a spot where you can see a mosque (once a church) in the foreground. Towering behind it is a government building—the tallest, most modern, ready-to-blast-off son of a bitch in the massive court. The old stones, deep arches, and clock tower hark back to the days of British and Ottoman control, while the new Israeli government building, less than 60 years old, speaks of the Western way of the Israeli state. It's the history of two nations in a glance.

But what the hell? I'm back. Here! On the Haifa highway with my surfboard—and all I can think is that madness lurks around the bend.

SURFING

He who experiences the surf engages the spirits of the gods.

THE SHEIKH

In surfing, the waters run deep with unspoken customs. In California, there's often this passive-aggressive thing out in the water, as surfers tend to give off a tough-guy stare and occasionally lay into each other with *language*. Sometimes they even trade blows. But it's mostly cheap theater: a last-ditch jerk of the animalistic brain that masturbates to its own brutish power. So my plan was to do the Israeli surfing thing on a low-profile basis—at least till I could gain some kind of footing, gauge the temperature, know the ringmasters who whipped the beasts at the local circus. But it could easily backfire.

Though I had briefly seen people surfing Haifa in the summer of 2007, I didn't surf there myself, so I really didn't know much about these Israeli surfers. It was all so new to me that on this return trip, I wanted to hang out with the Haifa surfers and learn what I could about the place. I wanted a dose of local knowledge that could save me from getting stung by a jellyfish, hit by a stingray, or fired upon by some fiendish Islamist militia. And besides, most surfers in the world like to paddle out with friendlies to ride waves. It's safer. More fun. But I had no idea whether these Haifa surfers would be willing to share their most prized asset with an unannounced dude from California. Would they ban me from their best spots? Would they run some kind of Israel Defense Forces kind of heckle on me? Perhaps they would see me as some soft American hebe, fresh off a Birthright Israel trip, leaving them no option but to make some kind of savage commando out of me. *After all,* I kept thinking, *this was the Middle East.* Just like the random kidnapping of Israeli soldiers that led to the outbreak of the 2006 war, anything could happen. At any time.

Some of those churning possibilities left me uneasy. Most of the time I felt great, on it, and in control. But there were moments when I wondered if my plan to surf the Middle East was simply too out there. My senses were not yet attuned to the world's most combustible region. I couldn't sniff out the difference between savage humor and approaching danger. I didn't know how to assume things. *Am I really prepared for the uncertainties of the Middle East? Have I wandered too far?*

Ahh . . . careful! Careful! That psychological twister can freak out even the most brazen of travelers. And for me, it could have been just the thing that prevented me from getting to know the Haifa surfers. After a brief hesitation, I shook it off, thinking, *Jesus, man, just go for it!*

So it was a moment of luck (and utter amazement) that as soon as my taxi pulled up to the Port Inn in downtown Haifa, a total stranger came running up to me with a phone—right on cue. No sooner had I jammed Che through the sea-rusted door of the Haifa guesthouse than the inn manager handed me the phone with his "buddy who surfs" on the line. *Was it really going to happen like this?*

"Hello?" I mumbled into his old brick of a cellular.

"Hi. My name is Lee. I heard you are . . . a surfer?"

I'll never forget Lee's ecstatic voice over the crackly cell.

"You came on *just* the right day, man. The waves are building to head-high and the wind is . . . do you want to meet at Carmel Beach?"

Two hours later I was trading off waves in the salty break of the Mediterranean with Lee—a cool Israeli I knew absolutely nothing about. But sweet hell, what did it matter? He was a surfer.

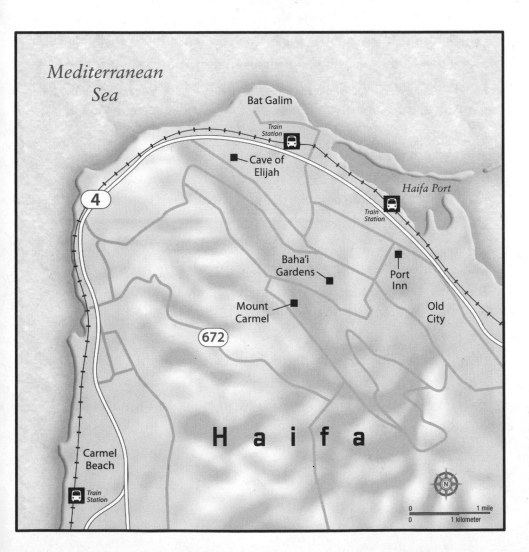

It was under the second lifeguard tower at Carmel Beach—just a few easy stops down that coastal railway—that Lee and I slapped hands, chatted, and agreed effortlessly that the surf was worth riding. It was so natural. None of that awkwardness you might think would come from walking into a situation as strange as this one. This was surfing.

"Whoa!" Lee exclaimed. "I see you brought your *own* board." He started inspecting the need-for-speed four-fin setup installed on Che's bottom half. His eyes were glued to Che like a craftsman to his tools. He slowly slid his sturdy hand down the side rail of the board, inspecting the taper of Che's feathered edge. Then he whipped him around, pausing to notice the notched swallowtail cut on the bottom of the board. Lee smiled with increasing approval. Then he flipped Che upside down, running his flat palm along the smooth bottom plane that would soon be polishing the warm sea-top.

"You know, I am a surfboard shaper," said Lee with a calm modesty. "This shape is something I've never seen here in Israel . . . it's perfect for our waves."

I shrugged. I muttered something about how my friend Dave Johnson of Progressive Surfboards designed the foamy thing for what we thought would be the smaller, weaker waves of the Mediterranean. But I swallowed the "smaller and weaker" bit; the waves were breaking with solid A-frame peaks, with near head-high sets. Not exactly a session in Dinkertown, Flatville.

I started to grin. Lee already was.

"Well, Lee," I burst out with excitement, "it's time to test the damn thing."

No nod required. The wild Israeli surf was waiting.

———

When the Mediterranean water first hit my toes, that warm liquid dissolved all the stress created by that *cus ima shelha* jackass from the taxi a few hours before. Sure, most seas of the world have this kind of refreshing feel, but there was a strong sense of historic mysticism here. There was a strange and epic feeling that This Moment was part of a long string of Past Moments that connected humanity on this northern Israel shore. Hell, the Cave of Elijah was just up the hill. *Behind me.*

The peaks-to-sea coastline of Haifa can sneak up on any unsuspecting dullard. It is easy to pass over the fact that the Prophet Elijah planned for the destruction of the pagan god Baal from the very Haifa cave that was just a craggy climb up the hill from the ankle-deep water in which I was standing. For a moment, I got a strange feeling that Elijah's ghost was hanging atop this Biblical cave, resting on an old slab of white rock, waiting, watching, gazing wearily out on the Haifa surf, into the horizon, and across the Mediterranean to that pagan lair on the highest mountain of Crete: the Cave of Zeus. Where I think Plato found his inspiration for the Allegory of the Cave. (Ever flip through *The Laws*?)

But this was no time to ponder the destruction of pagan gods. Surf takes priority. So Lee and I pounced on our boards and paddled through the bombardment of the break to the calm outer waters of the sea. We sat up and scanned fervently with our salt-stung eyes for the next meaty set to rise from the depths of the hazed horizon.

Growing restless out in the water, Lee turned to the 15 or so other Haifa surfers and casually bellowed something in Hebrew.

When I asked, Lee's casual translation went, "Guys! Guys! This is Jesse. He writes for a surfing magazine and is doing a story on surfing in Haifa."

Creeping Jesus! I thought. Sure, Lee was a dude, but what about the rest of these jackals? If I were to do in California what Lee did for me, I would be (a) chastised for bringing a nonlocal, (b) forever condemned for inviting some Random Rick (or Dick?) from the surf press, and (c) put on some kind of wave probation for assuming any of this wave-hog shit was kosher in the first place. *Yes, those California degenerates would have let me have it, all right . . .*

But these Haifa surfers were a different breed. They were fully cool with my being there. They didn't mind at all that a random dude from California just stopped on by . . . though the whole thing could have been different if they knew I'd soon be in Lebanon. With so much rage and anger along the Eastern Mediterranean from all that has happened I knew that there would be no room for an objective onlooker. There was no such thing as even being objective. So I had to be on everyone's "side." I couldn't count on my bumbling "dudeness" for protection. I would have to project parts of myself that I knew they'd want to be buddies with: the American with some Jewish blood. Nothing malicious. But it felt weird—like only part of who I was could be accepted.

On the El Al flight over, I had pondered the possibility of surfing with Israelis and wondered about the best way to handle it. If I said nothing and gave off my California "don't talk to me" vibe, I might get away with blending in as an Israeli. But Lee had announced me to the lineup. And for a good, long moment I waited to see what came next.

But strangely, I got no negative reaction from the Haifa

surfers. Most of them (ranging in age from 10 to 50) came over to greet me with welcoming smiles. "Shalom. My name is . . ." was how the next five minutes went. And it was all quite fine.

Israel is one of the few places in the world where nearly anyone can pass on the street as a citizen. Everyone has roots in another place and the liberal Israeli ethos lends itself to accepting nearly all styles and orientations. There is no "Jewish look" in Israel. It is a collection of looks that is known as Israeli. If you're still bewildered by this notion, email the Babylonians, Romans, or any other fuck-savage empire that scattered the Jewish people. Once, I even met a Chinese-looking dude who claimed to be Jewish. *(Strange . . . did I just type that, or think it?)*

But never, *ever* have I come across a more open and friendly band of surfers than in Haifa. These were not reactionary brutes, but young men like me, who enjoyed a life out in the water and a cold beer after. And more than anything, they just loved to offend the dreamy flocks of foreign Jews who had come to Haifa on the whim of an ancient pilgrimage. These uptight tourists would come from all over the former Eastern Bloc, America, and all places wealthy Jews can be found, for a romantic stroll along the Carmel Beach boardwalk in Zion. Many of them—or so one of the Haifa surfers told me during a hashish session in the beach parking lot—give a lot of money to Israel and expect everyone to live up to some kind of "proper" Jewish ethos. Many of them, so I was told, "only eat kosher in Israel, too."

The Haifa surfers knew exactly which buttons to push on the great Zionist machine. They had that mischief gene, all right—and nothing could have been more fun than portraying the coastline like it had been hijacked by a wild gang of ass-crack-wielding *thrillniks*.

THIS WAVE

If the doors of perception were cleansed every thing would appear to man as it is, infinite. For man has closed himself up, till he sees all things thro' narrow chinks of his cavern.

WILLIAM BLAKE

"Go! Go!" yelled a few of the Haifa surfers from afar. It was time. A wave was coming. Some old, pestering wave god from Crete had blown in a mounding swell that was starting to rise from the depths of the sea. The water had that green, clear, glassy look, and you could see right down through its crystals to the mysterious, volcanic bottom. But this maritime hump was starting to build, goddammit, taking shape and filling with size and power. The water below was sucking out to sea—a jolt of juice for the building crest, bringing the savage crags of reef *that much closer.*

And that's when the strange music starts. All of nature's factors have aligned to allow you, the surfer, to lunge yourself into the meat of this thrilling colossus. It is a serene moment. Rational thought caves in, as your animal brain, your adrenaline, takes over. So you paddle like hell down the mounting steepness of the developing face, knowing damn well the toil that awaits your body *if* you fall. All other things are in the background now, swallowed up by this mystically familiar tempo, the epic of the sea. Your later today, your tomorrow, your job, your spouse, even that motherfucker you bank with have all been made irrelevant by this looming moment: The Wave.

There is a *flash* of uncertainty when the great power of the sea grabs you, pulling the nose of your board into the full steepness of the crest, forcing you into a line you're not quite sure is even makeable. But so much for that. You've already *committed*. So you grab the rails and arch your back as your lead foot slides up the waxed deck, planting that twisted sucker down with Solomon-like authority. The rest of your body follows as you come upright, rushing down the line, parallel to the shore, setting up for the Perfect Ride.

The Perfect Ride. An *orgasm*. Known only to those who have actually had one. How could it be explained to a child? It must be felt. Earned. Which is fortunate, because this wave does start to kick, gaining speed as the water is hastily draining from your only makeable exits. It's chasing you, like a pack of rabid beasts, lurching and closing in fast. No margin for error.

Jesus God, you think. *Can I make it?*

With your knees breezed and your front foot lightly pumping, you hustle through this manic chase of whitewater destruction. Reality hits: the lip of the wave has started to break, *almost* over your head and into the curl. Nature's music is so humbling; a mere moment in this wave-covered "shack" seems like a blissful eternity. A moment that took years of preparation. For *this* sober moment. And it is now. Utterly sublime. The shack of . . . the source of . . . the Holy Grail. The peace humanity has overlooked on this Middle Eastern shore for thousands of years.

And it is all felt together: the Surfer, the Wave, the Perfect Ride, the Holy Grail, the Peace.

But only for a moment.

This ride is over.

Your adrenaline wanes as you slow into the calm periphery of the break. And you come to terms with the idea that you have come along with this wave—as if *you* were literally riding *it* . . . but were you?

ANCHORS AWAY

You're coming to realize that travel anywhere is often a matter of exploring half-understood desires. Sometimes, those desires lead you in new and wonderful directions; other times, you wind up trying to understand just what it was you desired in the first place.

ROLF POTTS

When Westerners first stumble upon the cultures of the Middle East, there's a feeling of "Creeping Jesus! Who are these people?" Flying into Israel is comparatively easier than landing in one of the surrounding Arab countries, as the Ashkenazi (European Jews) hold the power and ensure the general reign of the Western ethos. But none of this really matters—for whenever you think you can grossly categorize a chap into some kind of cultural group, he'll do something that's so beyond your wildest imagination that you end up trying to figure out what made you slap on that label in the first place.

Ah, yes . . . like when I first arrived in Haifa and tried to catch a cab. Just after Che and I had to deal with that *cus ima shelha* jackass, we stumbled down to the next one, which turned out to be an even more menacing experience.

Cruising along the Haifa coast, looking at Che as he rested flat on the front seat, I was starting to feel pretty comfortable. We were picking up speed, the ride was smooth, and we were moving freely along the open highway, just under the coastal escarpment of the Haifa hills. The windows were down. The sun was up. It was one of those glossy-adventure-magazine afternoons.

I spoke first, strategically. "Haifa is my favorite city in the north." Complimenting a local's turf can go a long way—especially as a dullard American, traveling with surfboard. The stereotype is that Yanks don't *really* appreciate Israelis' problems and are willing to throw money at any and every conflict in the region, as long as it goes away. And by "goes away," I mean off the front page of whatever tabloid-ridden, sub-intellectual, Sarah Palin–loving, sex-scandal-driven newspaper your typical "Don't burden me with the facts" American chooses to wake up to in the morning.

"Yes . . ." he said, pausing for a liberal five one-thousands. "Yes, Haifa is my favorite city, too." The cabbie's slow tempo gave him an unmistakable old-man quality that matched the leisure of his driving.

I continued, my arm casually draped across the back of the seat, my leg resting atop the open middle cushion. "Yeah, I like the trees, the hills, the sea, the waves—I really like how Haifa is a city where you can get a good piece of *kunafa*."

"Ahh, *kunafa*," he said. "The *only* thing Arabs are good for."

My eyebrows lifted in startled disbelief. Before I could fully process the sharpness of his intolerant tongue, his soft whisper twisted into a scratchy snarl—a guttural and wretched howl—as if I had wandered into some strange Oriental dynamite factory that just randomly exploded!

"That is why I voted for *Lieebürrmann!* I don't even want to *smell* the Arabs!" His right hand waved wildly in the air. "Why don't they just get out of Israel and go where they belong? This is Jewish land!"

Stunned, I stammered, "Lieberman?" *Avigdor Lieberman, the former nightclub bouncer? The founder of the far-right Yisrael Beiteinu party? I mean, the goddamn foreign minister!?! Jesus. What a fanatic.*

"Yes, *Lieebürrmann*. The *only* Israeli politician you can trust!" His whole arm was wavering to the jig of hysteria, and like a tenured professor, his manifesto was at hand. "All you American Jews—you are Jewish, my boy?—yes, all you Americans *think* the Arabs need a state. But they already have states! That is why we *must* vote for *Lieebürrmann!*"

I couldn't help but light up the backseat with a deep smirk of amusement. I just loved how immediately this harmless old chap had turned into a nationalist nut—*all after a little risk-free comment on local pastry.*

But it was the way he said it: "*Lieebürrmann!!!*" As if Avigdor Lieberman were some kind of mysterious Frankenstein monster, in a mysterious tower, with mysterious electronic gizmos humming all around. When the gathering dark clouds ripened, they would burst a bolt that would strike the high tower, raining a charge upon an unconscious beast strapped to a wooden table. With a Slavic twang, the mad scientist would cry to his mad scientist friends, "Fire up the Lieebürrmann!!!" And the Arab-chasing Frankenstein would come alive. *Alive!*

Sure it was all too much. But what the fuck? This was the Middle East. Nearly all taxi rides are packed with spastic entertainment.

Though I was still attentive enough to make the looming connection at hand: this old man was not a sabra, or native of Israel. So I asked where he was from, hoping it would expose the roots of his *Lieebürrmann* rage.

"I was born in Latvia . . . long ago," he said, calming a bit—though I could still see the pulsating veins along his open neck. His blood was still boiling.

This Haifa cabbie was part of a near-million wave of Jewish immigrants who came to Israel the decade after The Union fell. For many reasons—brash Soviet oppression, anti-Semitism, the rabid feeling of being caged behind the Iron Curtain—these ex-Soviet Jews have had an extreme effect on Israeli politics. Their bloc is today considered to be both fiercely secular and fiercely nationalist. The 2009 election of Binyamin Netanyahu and his formation of arguably the most conservative cabinet in Israeli history helped to confirm this fact: the old days of those half-naked socialist kibbutzniks James Michener wrote about are damn-near kaput. *The Source* now parties in Tel Aviv.

And so Israel finds itself with a Frankenstein Lieberman foreign minister who campaigned on a platform forcing a Zionist loyalty oath upon approximately 20 percent of Israel's Arab population—nearly all of whom were literally born into the sovereignty of the Jewish state. But Lieberman was born in Moldova. And when you get Palestinian-Israelis going with a strong bottle, they'll even claim to speak better Hebrew than he does. "He is not *from* here," they will plead, waving their arms like a frantic loon. "Just listen to his accent!" Then you realize you've whipped them into a frenzy by lurching into the Most Sensitive Issue in the land—the 1948 creation of the Israeli state, or the *Nakba* ("Great Catastrophe") for the Palestinians—and you cut your losses and dart out the door like the freak that you are.

Communicating telepathically with Che on the front seat, I thought, *I hope this Latvian cabbie doesn't feel the need to escort me into the Port Inn—I can't remember, but it might be run by Arabs.*

Instead . . . that crabby old cabbie pulled a fast one on me. Like all scoundrel taxi drivers in Israel, this Latvian kept his meter hidden in the glove compartment. When I finally asked him to turn it on—no more than a quarter mile from the train station—he did, but upon arrival at the guesthouse he demanded I forfeit an extra 20 shekels (roughly $5.00) for the short, unmetered distance at the beginning. He even cited Che as an extra cargo charge. But of course I covered that Idealistic Ass.

———

When I got to Carmel Beach and the general spot where I was meeting Lee, I paused, holding Che upright, and let out a sigh of disappointment. The surf had dropped. I'd assumed the waves would be decent for at least a few days. In California a swell can last for up to a week. Depending on the season, sometimes longer. But this is unknown to The Giant Puddle. Its storms are smaller than those of the Pacific; its waves are always running out of open water to build on. This makes the swell period shorter. More choppy. Not the crisp, big-wave conditions you'd see on the front of a surf magazine. But surfing is the kind of sport where you pull up to a place, and if you don't completely ditch all the responsibilities in your life to paddle out, you rest easy, knowing the conditions are either going to get better . . . or worse. I always liked this about the sport. Not everything in life is so *luxuriously* black or white.

And so with the sea rather small, I looked down the boardwalk of Carmel Beach and saw Lee's uncle and his buddy Dawnty, getting stuff ready for some roguish sea adventure.

When I walked over to them I asked what they were doing, and the reply went something like this: "Well, Jesse, the surf's flippin' flat . . . and I don't really feel like working today. Plus, Lee claimed he saw an anchor out in the sea a few days ago when he was 'just paddling around.'"

So, our mission would be to recover it.

It was just the kind of spine-tingling thing my buddies and I would pull back in California. It was as adventurous as it was deviant, and I knew I wanted in . . . even though I thought it would be a goddamn Hanukkah miracle if we found the thing. But what the hell? So Lee and Dawnty hopped on two kayaks, and Lee's uncle and I jumped on two haggard boogie boards. We hooted like adolescents and waded through the weak breakers in search of lost treasure.

A few hundred yards out, I peered down through the water of the calm Mediterranean. The midday sun illuminated the water with a turquoise transparency that made me feel like I was on some majestic dive off the waters of Aruba. But down through those simple shades of excellence, I saw only an aquatic desert. No anchor. Just sand, with ripples bending along the sea floor.

"What are your lineup points onshore?" I kept hollering to Lee. But he only grinned—not breaking from his "almost there" cunning. Dawnty started to ride him about it, too. But in Hebrew. Lee's uncle didn't seem too concerned. He was quiet—just another stoic out in the stoke of the sea. And just when it seemed we were as likely to find the anchor as to end up on some sexy nymph-inhabited island near Lesbos, Lee shouted, "Here! Here!"

The Haifa surfer flipped his kayak in fury, going for full effect as he gave off another asylum-worthy howl. *Ahh, Jesus! Here we go!*

Dawnty started yelling, too. "I see it! I see it!"

I looked down, but it wasn't until I masked myself and dove a respectable ten feet that I could distinguish the historic anchor. *How the hell are we going to get this old thing up? It must be 20 feet down.*

Again, Lee surprised me. He came up, flipped his kayak right side up, and called to Dawnty to sling him the ropes. Evading our questions really had the desired effect: we were blown away. I looked at Lee's uncle, and he lifted his brows in a sort of big-deal stun. "Whoa!" is what he wanted to say, but he fell short of the word.

Not wasting a moment, Lee started tying the rope into one of the drain holes on Dawnty's kayak. He planned to tie the bottom of the rope to the anchor, and then roll the kayak until the anchor was lifted from the sand. Impressed, Lee's uncle paddled over to secure the kayak like he had some mysterious understanding of the operation. *Had he known all along?* Dawnty and Lee's uncle tended our crafts as we dove to make the pivotal knot on the anchor.

Sinking in the Mediterranean Sea takes more effort than in the Pacific Ocean. The salt makes you float like a buoy and it sucks your fluids like an Amazonian mosquito. So when we hit the anchor, we were already ready to come up. I tried to quickly move the iron hunk, but nothing. I needed air. It was an effort just to stay so far below the surface. I started to rise—but I kept looking down as Lee lassoed the thing, darted up, and exploded through the surface of the water a mere moment after me. We were gasping for air. But we had our knot.

"Did you get it? Did you get it?" Dawnty asked frantically.

"Roll!" cried Lee, panting like a champion. It was a clever maneuver—something that surely would have shocked the squares along the Carmel Beach boardwalk.

We muscled the kayak like madmen, rolling the rope around the hull to lift the anchor out of the sand. But the bugger was in there all right, and the kayak was wobbly. Dawnty slipped and let out a strange cry that should only be described as *unique*. We all laughed and cussed a bit. *Cus ima shelha!*

On our second try, we twirled the anchor out from the sand. But it was too heavy to bring to the surface. So we hauled it a few feet off the sea bottom as we swam our sorry flotilla back to shore.

"Leeee!" I called, out of breath. "Whose anchor is this?"

"I dunno," he called back. "It's British. No, French." *Man! He doesn't know.*

Nearing the beach, we lifted the back-torquin' thing through the small breakers and plopped it onto a dry splotch of sand. Gawking tourists were starting to gather in amazement. It would have been classic if we started speaking some strange tongue, like we had been wandering the sea for thousands of years—lost sailors from Homer's story.

"Ha!" Lee exclaimed. "Look at them . . . they think we're crazy!"

"Think?" I joked.

"Look at all that stuff on it," Dawnty said, reaching out for it. "How do you say this in English?"

"Umm . . ." I paused. "Coral?"

It looked like your classic Popeye the Sailor anchor. It was simple in design, with a deep set of U-shaped claws, dressed with years of fascinating sea life. Brown coral with greenish shells and wormlike rock spirals hinted that this anchor had been sitting there for a long, long time.

A few months later when I was living in West Beirut, I got an email from Lee: "Jesse! Some professor at Haifa University came to look at the anchor today. Dude, it's over 1,000 years old!"

It was a King Hell Bastard of a find.

DÉTENTE: ONE WAVE AT A TIME

When a jackrabbit gets addicted to road-running, it is only a matter of time before he gets smashed—and when a journalist turns into a politics junkie he will sooner or later start raving and babbling in print about things that only a person who has Been There can possibly understand.

HUNTER S. THOMPSON,
Fear and Loathing: On the Campaign Trail '72

After stashing the anchor and trading off meager, waist-high waves in the Carmel Beach lineup, Lee and I took our last wave all the way in to the shore. We were parched. The desert-fed salt of the Mediterranean Sea had nearly sucked us dry, purging our moisture glands with a Dead Sea kind of intensity. My eyes stung, badly—and knowing the feeling well, Lee suggested we go by his friend Raouf's house for a drink.

After a stroll along the boardwalk, we walked behind an old rock house that spoke of nothing in this century. To the trained eye, this house read of Ottoman-controlled Palestine. That was the hint . . . because when the door opened, Raouf boisterously welcomed us in *Arabic*, then turned to Lee and welcomed him boisterously in Hebrew. And I just stood there. *Was it all some kind of joke?*

Raouf was like Lee in many ways: in his late 20s, working as a part-time lifeguard, with a fine-tuned sense of smartassery that was often exercised on the boardwalk. The difference was that Raouf actually lived here, literally. Less than an eight-iron golf shot from the sea.

—

And like the hospitable Arab surfer he was, Raouf pleaded with us to rest our boards near his front door and walk out on the second-story roof that doubled as a deck. Raouf pulled up three chairs for us, excused himself, and walked back into his kitchen.

"I go way back with Raoufy," Lee said casually, stretching his arms way above his head, looking out in the direction of the sea. "We used to party together. Surf together. Everything, man. He's one of my best friends."

I heard a blender fire up. Raouf was still in the kitchen. I hunched a bit closer to Lee. "It's not a problem that he's an . . . *Arab*?"

Astonished, Lee dropped his arms and emitted an Arabian-strength guffaw. "Hey, Raoufy . . . Raoufy!"

Out the door came Raouf, carrying three iced drinks with freshly-cut celery stalks planted into the blood-red juice of blended vegetables.

"Raoufy," Lee called, "is it a problem you're a *dirty* Arab and I'm a *stingy* Jew?"

"Yes. It is a big problem," Raouf replied, emphasizing his Arab accent with pronounced seriousness. Then both Raouf and Lee roared with laughter. "Seriously, though," Raouf started, taking a seat, "there are many problems here. I am half-Lebanese, half–Dutch and Catholic." He paused to look Lee over skeptically. "And Lee, well . . . he is half from Baghdad, and half from Europe. And when you look at it that way, we're both half-Arab and half-European. So we're like brothers. The same, yes?"

I had never really thought of it that way. In fact, it was just the kind of cheese-dick story I would have expected to hear from some liberal from the International Solidarity Movement in an East Jerusalem café. I would have felt obliged to ruthlessly counter, "No. Arabs in the Middle East—and particularly Jews—just don't see themselves like *that*." But who was I? An actual Arab and an actual Jew—in the goddamn Middle East—were telling me their friendship went beyond the "conventional feudalism." They were surfers.

Raouf raised his deep brows. "Sure, there are problems . . . this is the Middle East! But look what we have here." He pointed toward the aquatic trance of the Mediterranean. Between the cones of pine trees, we could see the white sandy beach. Beyond it, the molten ball of the sun slid into the horizon and cast a shimmering golden carpet across the sea.

"This," the Arab said, "is what binds us."

THE KNOLL OF THE ROCKET

Yes, it is true our fighters shot 4,000 rockets into the Zionist project. We did it so that South Lebanon can now attract unemployed California surfers to our part of the Eastern Mediterranean.

HASSAN NASRALLAH,
Secretary General, Hezbollah

All along the Eastern Mediterranean there are harrowing extremes. On this divided coast, beauty runs just as deep as the illness of conflict. It's something almost as timeless as the sea; nobody really knows when it started or why, or if it even has the capacity to go away. All people know is that it exists, in this moment of time . . . and its reminders are ever present, with the ability to sneak up on you, awakening your brain and tuning your senses to a brutish reality not natural to the California surfer.

And so it was like a methadrine-crazed bat that Lee darted out of his small Japanese four-cylinder car and ran across the pothole-ridden road. "C'mon!" he yelled. He had offered to give me a ride back to the Port Inn after hanging at Raouf's house, but suddenly he turned off the main road.

Darkness had just set in—and there was wild and random brush scattered across the mysterious terrain that was hard to make out. Dull silhouettes of rock formations were spread across the path, giving off an eerie, time-capsule ambience, as if we'd driven into a 100-year-old David Roberts watercolor of Ottoman Palestine.

"C'mon, Jess!" Lee called, nearly running now. "I want to show you something!"

So I started after him, away from the light and up the shadowy knoll. The air felt warmer here than at the beach—thick, rich, exactly how the Nazis of any college English department would want the word *Mediterranean* to work as an adjective. The grass was squishy, growing darker as I trampled over its long shadows. As I ran, my shorts left my legs open to hitting random weeds and bushes. Potentially hostile creatures could have been lurking in the dark, ready to spring or pounce or whatever the hell such *unknown things* do in that part of the world. *Were there snakes on the hillside? Maybe an unexploded landmine from an early Arab-Israeli war?* I didn't have time to think. And the faster I moved, the more I felt vulnerable to realties I didn't yet know existed.

By the time I caught up to the madman, I had worked myself into a state of twisted passion. *What happened to going back to the Port Inn? What was this Goddamn Fucking Surprise!?*

Lee had stopped, panting, at the top of the dark and grassy knoll. He turned back to wait until I came up beside him. "Look down!" he ordered.

I did. Briskly. Ready for the worst.

But to my surprise, I saw nothing.

"No!" he said sharply. "Look here!" He pointed, forcefully. And his voice was commanding, like it had been cast from an iron den of institutional authority—the army? I wasn't used to hearing my newly palled surf mate speak in such a way. This was serious. But what did it mean?

Lee pointed with both hands, callused from their daily duties of surfboard shaping. And then I saw it: a gnarled pipe was sticking up out of the ground a few feet. I hadn't noticed it as I ascended the knoll. *Okay, a stray pipe. Had we really run all the way out here for a pipe?*

And *zap*—like a punch to the face—the reality hit like a boxer without gloves: these guys were messing with me, setting up some kind of Israeli joke on me! The American. I jerked my body around, scanning fervently for the surf jackals ready to pounce. But something seemed off. I couldn't get it. And it was Lee, the way he looked at me through the shadowy dark—a glance of dire warning, as if my life could soon be wavering in the balance.

Had I gotten these Haifa surfers wrong? Had they just been playing along with me, waiting for the right moment to beat the hell out of this Californian?

There was no way to describe the panic I felt. I was alone and only a few weeks into the Middle East, and I hadn't quite adapted to the subtleties of this climate. *What if I had misread the character of these guys, who most of the time seemed so much like me?*

Mad waves of bewilderment were now bombarding the tissues of my speedy cortex. *What had I gotten myself into?* The fear had sunk into me, standing on top of the knoll.

Looking at me in the twilight, Lee saw that his Goddamn Fucking Surprise had left my mind reeling with fear. He seemed confused by this but shrugged it off, and went back to the feeling that caused me to freak.

He spoke in a sober voice. "This metal pipe used to be attached to a sign. In 2006, a rocket from Lebanon hit this sign." Lee's gruff hands were playing out a shadow drama with the stubby pipe.

Lee pointed at the ground beneath my feet. "Right where you are standing was a hole." Then his deep-set eyes twisted toward mine as he uttered the name that gave me The Fear: "Hezbollah."

We both fell into silence.

His expression slowed the tempo of my heart. This was a matter of life and death. But it wasn't about me. I had only misinterpreted Lee's grim seriousness because I wasn't *from* Haifa; I wasn't used to surfing with the very real possibility that *rockets* could land on the very soil where I was standing. They could hit anywhere, at any moment. As they had in the 2006 war.

In California, there is no rocket threat and it would be ridiculous to even think of it. Clearly, Lee had caught on to this. He sensed that I was only enjoying myself like a houndish surf mutt, not tuned in to the guarded Middle East manner that defines a Haifa surfer. And that irked him—but not in any mean or malicious way, just enough to make him wheel his small Japanese four-cylinder off the main road and give me a goddamn heart attack by showing me the knoll of the rocket.

Very much unlike California surfers, Haifa surfers live under constant duress, a wrenched tightening in their gut that reminds them that this Eden of summer surfing is an illusion— there is no peace along the Eastern Mediterranean. Lee knew it would have been a crime to allow a California surfer to see only the lucid waves and *not* the red paint that makes Haifa a target for random rocket fire. Fifty miles north were an estimated 50,000 Hezbollah rockets in South Lebanon. They were pointed at every Israeli place I describe.

Since arriving in Haifa, I had been so locked into my "duder" vibe that pondering the toils of the Middle East seemed absurd. It wasn't till that night on the knoll that the haggard truth hit: we were surfing in Rocket Country.

My mind checked back in the middle of Lee's explanation about how the sky was particularly open to the Lebanese north here. And yes, this elevated knoll had taken one of the 4,000-plus rockets Hezbollah launched in the 2006 war.

"All these little holes in the tree . . ." Lee broke the silence, showing me the holes left from the exploding ordnance. And then he paused—switching to his own dimly lit nightmare from the summer of 2006. "When the war started I was at my parents' house. We were eating dinner when the first rocket fell . . . it hit somewhere down the street. We all knew what it was because we'd been warned by Army Radio that Hezbollah had captured a few of our soldiers. It was war.

"Israel always goes to war for its soldiers," he continued. "But we didn't know how big . . . how many rockets. I went outside my house and looked far down the street along the Haifa waterfront and saw the smoke. Then I heard something. *Another rocket*, I thought. So I dove behind one of those green dumpsters and took shelter as it came crashing onto the street, hitting a parked car on my block just a few meters away from me. I was *that* close!

"You *gotta* remember, man, those Katyusha rockets are not guided for a reason . . . they are meant for us. The civilians."

During the 2006 war, I was glued to the TV, reading all the live reports I could find. Hezbollah and Israel both let each other have it, hitting at their most valuable commodities: their civilian populations. Standing next to Lee, I felt an emotional blast that couldn't be felt from California . . . in all its mind-blowing shock.

I had tasted the fright of war in Nablus, the West Bank, when I was there in 2007. But I thought I had grown hard to the Middle East—that it couldn't affect me this second time around.

But I was wrong. There was no way to surf the Middle East and not get lured back into all the grit of this place. It's a ghost that would appear at the most critical moments, across all lines, no matter whom I had yet to meet on either side of the Israeli-Lebanese border. It was something that was stuck in me.

———

That night I slept uncomfortably. Not because the communal bunks of the Port Inn were anything bad—they were actually quite good—but because something still irked me about Lee and the knoll of the rocket. Something about the unexpectedness of it all. How old memories could just come crashing back through my head, with no conscious awareness that they were even still lodged in my brain. The abrasive clash was so striking, so clean . . . so reminiscent of what I'd felt two years ago when I was in that apartment in the northern West Bank city of Nablus.

Those memories of the West Bank in 2007 hit me hard, whisking me back to the nightmarish scene, which I relived in a constant state of yesterday. When I returned to California I spent countless nights feeling sick to my stomach. I would sit alone in my San Diego apartment, waiting for the nine o'clock hour to hit, when fucking goddamn SeaWorld would blast its brazen fireworks and break the calm of the night sky. The explosions of Nablus all over again: the *gruuummmbllle* from the SeaWorld crowd was the convoy, the boom from the flare was to alert the Old City, the sizzling crackle was the Kalashnikovs of Palestinian gunmen as they fell from the savage waste of it all. My angst never lifted until the fireworks stopped. Even then, I would walk out on the porch and wait for a sniper to appear along the San Diego skyline. But he never came.

On those nights, I would end up in the shower, seizing the walls as my mind wandered like a soul lost in hell. Menacing flashbacks were lurking deep then. *Steam the water hot, motherfucker! Boil the sickness from my pores!*

After Lee's little adventure, I tossed and turned, falling in and out of sleep for the rest of the night. The horror Lee showed me had awakened a beast that claimed sovereignty over my soul: rockets in Haifa, snipers on rooftops in the West Bank, and Israeli convoys blasting through the Nablus casbah.

It was all just too much.

DELIRIUM OF DISORDER

I've seen the horror, the horrors that you've seen . . .
Horror and moral terror are your friends. If they are
not, then they are enemies to be feared.

COLONEL KURTZ,
at the top of the river, *Apocalypse Now*

It was like a band of werewolves that we would sit out on the porch and gaze into the glow of the Nablus casbah. There were four of us on those nights in June 2007: me, a WASPy Texan I would come to call As-Salibi, Adam the Brit, and The Third. By birth, he was Stewart Johonnot Oliver Alsop III, but I just called him "The Third." I'd met The Third while studying abroad a few months earlier. We traveled together through Turkey, the United Arab Emirates, Armenia, Georgia, and Israel and ended up in a strange apartment, working for a small NGO, in Nablus. We were white males. In our early 20s. We were invincible.

And so it was on that particular night, as the yellow moon crept over the valley walls, that we felt tricked with a familiar adrenaline, charged by the glow that was bombarding the moonlit city. We could feel that Nablus was about to come alive again—transforming us with a frightening jolt of guerrilla warfare.

Earlier in the day, Palestinians from our volunteership had described the nightly Israeli raids as "worse" than before. But nobody seemed to know why. The game was simple: Palestinian guerrillas would hide in the ancient alleys of the layered casbah while the Israelis raided it, arresting anyone who made them feel uncomfortable.

We later learned that on February 25, 2007, a few months before we arrived in Nablus, the Israeli Army had launched a wide-scale military attack, openly firing on civilians and arresting over 150 people, making it the largest operation in three years. Israeli forces occupied a number of homes, attacked local TV and radio stations, obstructed the movement of medical personnel, and placed a curfew on the city that flattened whatever was left of the local economy. None of us in the apartment knew this at the time, but we were learning fast.

From the porch of our high-rise apartment, overlooking the casbah, As-Salibi stood up from his chair and surveyed the scene. He brought a bottle of one of his nonalcoholic beers to his lips and took a healthy swig. Alcohol was forbidden in Nablus for "Islamic reasons." Taking another swig, he pointed out the balcony and said, "Isn't it just *nuts* that so many of the suicide bombers from the Second Intifada came from right over th—"

CRACK, CRL, CRL, CRACK!!!

Rolls of bombardment, laced with thunder, came crackling through the casbah. *Jesus God!* My mind broke from deliberation and flung recklessly into gear. *It was here!*

As-Salibi laughed in a sort of cathartic horror. Adam the Brit chimed in. The Third stood silent and perfectly still. I clutched the porch rail, bracing myself. The night's devilish overture was upon us.

"Okay, okay," As-Salibi started, attempting to calm the situation. "Okay, this is nothing. The Palestinians do this to alert the city when the Israelis are coming. It's just a firecracker. A fucking firecracker, man!" As-Salibi had been in this Nablus apartment a few weeks longer than the rest of us and I trusted his narration.

On cue, a moment later, the *gruuummmbllle* of an Israeli convoy came blasting past our building. *Christ, some loon had radioed in the jeeps. That Salibi bastard was right! The Israelis were coming!*

I froze on the balcony, struck by the shock of the invading convoy. Without a better place to hide, Adam the Brit ran inside and jammed closed the curtains. On instinct, The Third hit the deck. As-Salibi, with a rogue knee-jerk, kicked over his nonalcoholic beer, soaking The Third's pants as he lay on the floor, trembling like a junkie off his fix.

"Aww, man!" The Third groaned, wiping at his pants and getting back up.

"Shh!" Adam whispered from behind the curtains. "Quiet!"

The convoy passed. We could hear it rolling away toward the casbah. It was good to know that the raiding Israelis weren't after us, though technically, they could've been. Under the terms of a standard Israeli tourist visa, we weren't supposed to be in Nablus—but there *were no visas* for volunteering in the West Bank. So we just went, knowing that while it was unlikely, we still could have been targets of a deportation raid. Why not? The Israelis didn't want us in Nablus. The last thing they wanted was for Westerners to see the occupation . . . and write about it. Hell, they could've arrested us on the grounds of "security" and no more questions would have been asked.

Back in the apartment, we could barely hear the rumble of the convoy off in the distance. They were deep into the casbah now and their signature blended well into the chaos of the Nablus night. But I wondered how long the Israelis could remain before the Old City came down on them—before a masked militiaman unloaded an RPG onto their convoy. In my mind's eye I could see green-suited Israeli commandos kicking in the door to a house, tearing some Palestinian man out of bed and throwing him into the back of their jeep, only to be surrounded by a livid . . .

Bam! Bam! Bam! Sprays of machine-gun fire echoed through the walls of the casbah. *It happened. The militias were fighting back!*

We should have stayed inside . . . but we didn't. As-Salibi nudged his way through the curtains and shuffled back to his plastic chair for the view. Adam the Brit, The Third, and I followed, but slowly, with some serious goddamn reservations. But all we saw was the still glow of the Old City.

"Christ," I whispered under my breath. "We can't be drawing *any* attention up here. Stay low!" But we had to stay high enough to *see*. What if something happened? We had come too far to miss it.

While waiting for the convoy to return, The Third shared a thought that had been wearing on him. "I think we're in the apartment of some professor from An-Najah University," he said, laughing a little. "I opened the closet today and found a bunch of Hamas scarves and keffiyehs and stuff. Wouldn't it be fuckin' great if the Israelis—America's best friend—busted in our door and found us watching *this shit*, drinking nonalcoholic beer with a bunch of Hamas . . ."

"Ahh!" burst As-Salibi, in a craze. "Get inside! Hit the lights!"

We all rushed in and crouched on the floor, hoping to stay out of the line of incoming fire. I quickly flicked off the light, not completely sure what As-Salibi had reacted to. "They're coming back!" he said, louder than he should have, as the four of us rose a little and peered—ever so slightly—out the curtains for a look. I could feel my knees shivering with fear.

Whatever that gunfire down the street was about, it must have turned them around. The convoy was headed back along the street, just below our apartment building. But my guess was that they wouldn't even notice us from the street, as we were fortified in a mostly vacant building, with a broken elevator. Our balcony was one among dozens. As long as we didn't catch their attention, we should have been fine . . . but still, I was on Edge. I broke from formation and pressed my body against the buzzing wall as the convoy rumbled past, like a hell-bent tremor from the depths of the casbah. *Please don't let them stop here.*

Then the Israelis were gone. It was as if all of Nablus had been holding its breath. The tension released. Utter confusion broke out. Wailing Palestinian mothers were now the dominant force in the airwaves. I could hear them howling in public outbursts of hysterical angst—as if the past twenty years of nurturing their children had just been gunned down with one hellish bullet.

From every corner of the apartment I heard their cries.

And then . . . The Surreal kicked in, hitting my veins like a junkie who found the Spike. I could feel it spread—*slowly*—from one point to all over the meat of my crude matter; and then—*zap!*

Manic waves bombarded my system as everything started to rapidly shift gears: methadrine! All of us were blathering like psychostimulant-using freaks, gnawing on some organic adrenaline gland and chewing its charged fibers, allowing us to fly free in a world filled with gravity. *What had just happened? Why was I talking so fast?*

Ambulance sirens everywhere: Up! Down! Random trucks starting and stopping and screeching to the beat of chaos. People were taking action. Everywhere. The response was underway.

All in sync with The Rush . . . The Rush of War. Nothing synthetic about it. A couple of seconds felt like days, locked into the wavering dance of a savage fiend. And then, finally, it broke.

"Don't laugh," I harshed upon the boys. "Somebody probably just died."

They stopped. Now they were down. A little *too* down. As-Salibi turned to us. "Guys, be very, very quiet. Stop talking." He was looking out the window, not down to the street, but higher . . . and his face had turned pale.

I could taste my urge to vomit.

Climbing the stairs in the windowless building across the street was a dark silhouette, strangely transparent, as the glow from the casbah transformed his figure into a werewolf goon. We saw him creep through the gutted windows. As he ascended the rotisserie staircase, his outline became ever more clearly defined . . . that thing he carried was a rifle.

"Gah!" gulped Adam the Brit. "Fuck" had lost its punch. This situation was beyond words.

So we just sat there, quivering in fear as this haze-lit figure moved into a dark position. "You guys think . . ." Adam the Brit started, but he bit his tongue.

The manic wave of adrenaline was only a memory now. We took shifts watching the werewolf sniper, waiting deep in the building across from us. We spent the rest of the night coming up with reasons why this sniper—like the Israeli convoy—wouldn't see us as targets. But we kept our eyes on him, just as he—for all we knew—was keeping his eyes on us. Sides were hard to understand and everything was gray—as is often the case with noncombatants in war. We were just there.

Before the new day's sun crept over the valley walls and through the peepholes in our curtain from the night before, I managed to doze off for a good 30 minutes. It had been a bad night. And it officially ended when our landlord, Gingy, scared the Goddamn Bejeezus out of us by pounding on our door at dawn. He was armed only with Arabic coffee.

———

Later that morning, the man in charge of our NGO called As-Salibi to let us know we had the day off. "Like a vacation," Salibi repeated. So the plan was to stay low for a while. Let things clear a bit and wait out the violence. Until whatever was happening to Nablus blew over. If it even could.

We didn't worry about showering; nobody in the city had for days. A blown water main gave us all cover from this pungent bummer. And I don't remember any complaining. We were just too interested in what was going on—a brutal desire to get out and do what some crazed anthropologist would call "primary research." Angst was now our junk—our obsession.

Then As-Salibi hit us with the idea to venture into the city. "Get a little water and then hunker down for the heat," he said. I nearly freaked.

We are stuck in a city with no water and closed military checkpoints, and a goddamn heat wave is coming? Jesus, man, there are turds in the toilet! My nerves were nearly shot.

But As-Salibi got The Third and me motivated; Adam the Brit stayed in the apartment. So the three of us took the stairs down to the same street the Israeli convoy had nearly split in its screeching pre-dawn chaos.

"Put on your vests," said As-Salibi.

We were given vests by our NGO to wear when we needed to go into Nablus. But everyone in the city must have known what we were doing there, as there had been few wandering *gringos* since the thunder of the Second Intifada . . . but still, precaution was a good thing.

Our vests were printed with Arabic script and a strange, unrecognizable picture. To hell with the picture; As-Salibi, who could read Arabic, said the words amounted to "Aid Worker." *But was it enough?* We were about to walk through a situation too raw for the vest god's protection; and we were headed in the direction of the casbah. Salibi slowed his stumble and started to speak.

"Okay, guys, so it's probably a good idea to *not* laugh or smile here. Gingy said a few people died last night, so it would just be the respectful thing to do."

The Third and I needed no arm-twisting here. No extra convincing. We were in our own primal state of shock and horror; and when we came upon that quiet corner of hanging shrubbery, As-Salibi joined us in raw terror. "Ohh . . ." Salibi blurted. It was clear. We were standing in front of the iron gate of a cemetery. And there were people inside. It was still before nine o'clock a.m. *The bodies from last night's raid couldn't be in the ground already, could they?* But *our* casualty was truth. And in our skewed reality, the jangled lens that defined the doors of our perception, these *were* the bodies from last night's firefight.

"I know this sounds crazy," As-Salibi said, shaking himself straight, "but you guys wanna walk through?"

I scolded the Texan like a grandmother. But then . . . I felt my curiosity tingle. "Do you think it'll be safe?" *Were we addicted? Hopelessly lost in the spiral?*

This was madness—the kind of thing only someone who had been on the porch last night could understand. We knew we were hooked; yet we couldn't stop wondering as Wonderland twisted closer, tumbling down the rabbit hole of doom.

"Yeah, it's still early enough," said As-Salibi, shrugging. "Just don't make eye contact and we really shouldn't talk till we're out."

The Third and I nodded. Together we inhaled and exhaled the last deep breath we would take and started in from the street corner. We passed through the black rods of the cast-iron gate. We were inside. At first I looked down only at flat rocks on the sunken path. But then, up a little. *There must be hundreds and hundreds of graves here. Jesus, man, is this the place for everyone, or just martyrs? What if someone stops us and realizes I have a Jewish name? Ahh! I'll be a martyr!*

My mind was treading aimlessly with delirious thoughts, as riotous emotions reigned freely upon the Earth. I was questioning the most underlying tenets of my epistemology. *How do I know anything anymore? What is right?* Everything was more complicated.

The Third and I were still following As-Salibi, though more on his heels now. We were close and I pulled my vest tight, as if to signal that we were friendly to anyone who would notice. As-Salibi stopped. We were at a grave. Recently-turned clumps of soil and mounds of fresh flowers were sitting alongside a picture of some kid—*perhaps my age? 23?* He had a gun and a headband, both painted with Arabic calligraphy of Koranic script.

"Just a kid, man," I whispered, though to no one in particular. "Just a fucking kid."

As-Salibi nudged me back into silence, and we kept walking through the freshly stoked graveyard. I could hear Palestinian women wailing again. They were somewhere beyond the trees.

———

A few days later, with the violence still escalating, I left our Nablus apartment and pleaded with the Israelis to let me through the Hawara Checkpoint, which had been sealed to contain the violence—spilling over to surface streets in broad daylight. They eventually did. And a few days after that, when I was back in California, I saw this headline in a local newspaper: "Palestinian Parties Clash: Fatah Takes West Bank, Hamas Takes Gaza Strip."

It was commonplace to have Israeli-Palestinian clashes in Nablus, but we were there for the real menace: the Hamas-Fatah conflict, and the political infighting that divided the Palestinians from themselves.

THE BALLAD OF AS-SALIBI

The only way to deal with an unfree world is to become so absolutely free that your very existence is an act of rebellion.

ALBERT CAMUS

Sweet Jesus! Now, two years later, I was back in the Holy Land with As-Salibi. I knew it would happen someday. But of all places, I didn't think it would be in Haifa. When we parted in Nablus in 2007, the joke was that we'd see each other again on the set of our co-starring film, *Easy Rider: A Savage Motorcycling Quest Through the Syrian Desert* (or something like that). So, in other words, I hadn't the slightest idea when I'd see him again.

The truth about traveling (anywhere) is that you meet a lot of people. Anyone who has actually traveled—not merely been a tourist—will tell you this fact. There is something about sharing an innocents-abroad feeling that binds the most unlikely strangers in the most curious kinds of ways. But something always happens that ends these friendships (or sexships). The moment comes when people must go their separate ways. And then the question arises: *was I friends with this person because of the situation, or is there enough to maintain a friendship halfway across the world?*

The difference with As-Salibi and me is that Nablus 2007 wasn't your standard Italy abroad. This was the Middle East. The Palestinian Territories. Motherfucking combat on the streets. And the fright—our shared *experience*—had struck into us like a metallic sliver that never lost its sting. What As-Salibi and

I shared that summer was the mean, cold-blooded truth that not everyone on this planet is as lucky as we are.

———

In the end, As-Salibi and I kept our friendship. We were bound by an experience that had questioned everything we knew. And we needed each other. No Fraternity Frank could relate to what we saw—and endured—that summer in Nablus. We were convinced that our work in the Middle East would someday boom up the greatest seawall of our generation, and we knew that we were splitting the peak of a high and mighty wave.

So when the call came in from that WASPy Texan, I smiled, and answered with a sense of not-so-meek nostalgia.

"You'll never guess what happened the other day in Bethlehem," said As-Salibi, sounding tinny over his West Bank cell phone. "This guy at the office forgot my name, so, trying to get my attention, he called me 'As-Salibi.'"

As-Salibi means "The Crusader" in Arabic . . . as in a sword-wielding Frenchman from the Middle Ages. The term has enjoyed a bit of resurgence this decade, ever since another WASPy Texan (whose name is best left out of this saga) toppled two Muslim countries. But calling my buddy "As-Salibi" couldn't have been funnier. It was a hell of a nom de guerre, which was going to stick.

"So, yeah," said As-Salibi, with the same hysterical laugh I remembered from the porch in Nablus. "I've got the weekend off and I want to come to Haifa."

"Sounds great!" I said into my laptop. As with most Skype calls I made in the Middle East, I was ripping a random Internet connection from the airwaves, and for all anyone who could hear me knew, I was some sort of international spy, shouting into my computer about an assassination gone badly awry. Or at least it was fun to joke about with The Crusader. When the humor dries from a man—especially from a Middle East journalist—you know you have a problem. It's the ultimate indicator.

"Well, how's the beach?" Salibi asked eagerly. "Is it warm?"

"Warm? You Dumb Texas Bastard!" *Crazed laughter.* "It's hot! With waves. And naked frolicking girls everywhere . . . Jesus, man! It's Nablus!"

As-Salibi went wild. "Yeah?! Well, it's not exactly *Bethlehem,* either!"

A few hours later we were sitting on the Haifa beach, drinking Goldstar beer, enjoying the nearly naked Jewish Israeli girls as they flocked openly on their sanctuary along the shore. It was as if the lost Levantine fertility goddess Astarte had come down through the hills on her white horse and blown her magical kiss upon these hot-bodied beauties. It was sheer torment to exist as these Jewesses bounced with a natural lust that confirmed their ancestral roots in this land.

I rolled off my towel in overload. The hot grains of sand stung and confirmed I was actually alive.

━━━

Strange thoughts on that hedonist Haifa beach . . . but maybe not. Maybe I should have expected it all along: extreme emotions, balancing each other, extending in full orbit only to be reined back by the pull of the Great Magnet.

I rolled off the sizzling sand and back onto my towel. With my five-day-old whiskers holding the Haifa sand to my face, I carelessly mumbled to the Texan Crusader, "So, I told some of the Haifa surfers that you were coming to Haifa and my buddy Lee invited us to a party. Want to go?"

Salibi got *that look* in his eye. He was "The Party" in college, notorious for pulling all-nighters, only to demand a laptop—in full-spinning inebriation—at five a.m. to check the latest news out of the Levant.

"Are you kidding?!" Salibi said. "I'd *love* to go."

The Texan lived for working in the West Bank, but Jesus, man, the kid was still human. And the scantily dressed, inquisitive Israeli chicks were just the kind of occupation-buster As-Salibi needed to maintain his masculine sanity: the balance one needs for the meekness of traditional Bethlehem. "Even the Christians," he once said, weary of it all, "they're all just socially conservative."

We took the train back to the Port Inn—where As-Salibi was now staying, too—and phoned Lee that we were coming to his party. It was his birthday.

"Put an Israeli on the phone," Lee said through the Port Inn lobby phone. When I did, the inn manager scrambled for a pen and scribbled something in Hebrew.

"That," the inn manager said looking puzzled, "is what you need to show a taxi driver . . . this place your crazy friend told me is in The Hills."

The Hills?

Salibi gave me one of those Nablus-like nods, and I knew it was going to be a wild night.

GAZA MAID

Who is wise? The one who can foresee consequences.

BABYLONIAN TALMUD

"C'mon, man. This way," I called to The Salibi Crusader.

We were somewhere on a dark dirt path along the spiny Haifa escarpment and I was struggling to keep my balance, muscling a fiercely packed bag brimming with beer—the kosher Israeli stuff.

My normal policy when taking a taxi to an unknown place is *not* to let the sucker vanish until I can confirm that I'm in the right place. But we were stuck. The hysterical cabbie was in no mood for waiting and he demanded his shekels upon arrival. *Was this dimly lit dead end the place Lee told the inn manager on the phone?* The scene reminded me of the knoll of the rocket.

"Umm . . . I don't know, man," said Salibi. "Are you sure?"

From whatever lights existed below the escarpment, I pieced together that we were somewhere south of Haifa. *Maybe Carmel Beach?* I wasn't sure.

"I think," I called out to As-Salibi, "I think I can hear their drums and guitar." He was trailing me with growing uncertainty.

Lee had told me that for his birthday he wanted to have a "bonfire in the hills." But I had learned to be careful about filling in the blanks with my California bias. For all I knew, this was going to be a mutinous Israeli drum circle with deep nostril snortings of Yemeni khat.

Salibi broke in. "Dude, didn't this Lee guy say to take the

right fork after three minutes?"

"Ahh, Jesus," I moaned. "I can't remember! Let's just keep going until something happens."

We were well past the dead end of the street now, and a collection of endless small paths was splitting in all directions, reducing our unskilled navigation to luck.

It was one of those warm Haifa nights. We were dressed the same as nearly all Jewish Israelis: shorts, sometimes underwear, and a casual hippie T-shirt with sandals. And while this outfit may have suited the paved city blocks of downtown Haifa, we were now lost in the hills, trying to navigate a goddamn goat trail. The heat of the summer months had baked the water out of the surrounding vegetation, sharpening a myriad of prickly thorns that seemed to enjoy thrusting their javelin barbs through our ruined sandals. Still, no flicker of firelight.

"Damn it!" I yelled. Another prickler.

"Yeah," sympathized Salibi. His actions said "Fuck it," as he cracked open a beer. At least working on the West Bank hadn't taken The Party out of him.

When we finally got down the trail, we came upon a small plateau that opened naturally into the horseshoe mountainside. This was it. I could finally see the flickering flames of the bonfire.

At first glance, the party seemed to have plenty of beer, snacks, and longhairs playing African drums and acoustic guitar. Moving closer, I recognized Lee's uncle strumming in the light; his long blond hair and sunburnt nose made me smile: *This is exactly what you'd see in California.* But no word yet on the khat-snorting. Though I knew we'd get into that savage yak-herding stimulant soon enough.

"Whoa, the Americans! What's up, guys? Hard time getting down the trail?" he said, laughing.

"Oh, man," I replied, slapping his hand. "Thorns everywhere."

——————

While treading the path, As-Salibi and I started discussing exactly how we were going to explain ourselves to Lee and the Haifa surfers. On one hand, Lee and the gang were about the coolest and most understanding Israeli dudes I knew—and I was really starting to like them. On the other hand, this wasn't the Berkeley Free Speech Movement. Like telling a Christian fanatic you don't believe in God, crossing The Line on the whole Israel-Palestine thing tends to end friendships.

It was a dangerous truth that As-Salibi and I met in the West Bank city of Nablus in 2007, took Arabic in college, went to cultural events, read, blogged like junkies, and were now Middle East journalists. Neither of us wanted to lie—but what the hell were we going to say to this ex-army gang of Israeli surfers? "Well, hey, Lee, friends, this is my white, non-Jewish Texas buddy. I call him As-Salibi, 'The Crusader' in Arabic. I met this guy as perhaps some of you were raiding the Nablus casbah in 2007. You remember, when Hamas and Fatah militias were killing each other? Never mind. But you'll *like* this kid! Salibi now lives in Bethlehem and works for a Palestinian news agency. His job consists of reporting various human rights violations and war crimes your country allegedly commits . . . but no hard feelings."

Give me a break.

I had caught wind at a parking-lot hashish session that some of these Haifa surfers were freshly back from Operation Cast Lead, the January 2009 war in Gaza that resulted in over 1,400 dead Palestinians. They had danced with the devil that had taken them away from the Haifa surf and were on Serious Fucking Edge about it. They just weren't in the mood to sympathize with two American kids who wanted to hang out with Palestinians, or even hear about it . . . let alone my goal to surf from Israel to Lebanon. The truth—or even a flat version of it—would provoke a tension that didn't need to exist.

As-Salibi came up with something safe along the dirt path: "Say I work for a TV station in Jerusalem."

Sure. Why not? Everyone was probably drunk anyway.

So when As-Salibi and I jumped off the path to greet Lee, we passed through an easy introduction and followed the Baghdadi Jew over to his birthday party. It wasn't long till As-Salibi found some Israeli girls lounging on the hillside rocks in a way that no girl from Bethlehem would even consider. He helloed his way into the night. This was just the feminine jolt he needed. Not exactly in a sexual sense; it just reminded him that he was a refugee from the Western ethos that plays to the sexual deviant in us all.

One of the girls, who carried her robust, kibbutz-raised flesh licentiously, kept saying, "Wow, you guys are *so savatlan.*" Later, some drunk at the party told me that *savatlan* means calm and tranquil.

We small-talked with the girls for a while and then walked over to my bag to reload on beer.

It was then I saw one of Lee's buddies standing on an old ironing board like a surfboard, atop the ragged side of the craggy mountain. This escarpment went all the way down to the sandy shore of what I could now distinguish as Carmel Beach.

"Dooon't worrrry, guyyys," babbled the Buffoon. "I waaas in the arrrmy!" He wasn't a big kid, but he had that small-man glimmer of conviction that—along with the booze—convinced me he was actually going to slide down the mountain on the ironing board.

"My God!" I exclaimed to Lee. "What the hell is he doing?"

We raced over. Lee rapidly tried to talk sense into the Buffoon, but the drunken fool had already gone home with self-destruction. The two Israeli girls, Lee, Lee's uncle, As-Salibi, and a few other Haifa surfers crowded around in a counterproductive hysteria.

The fool had whipped the crowd into a frenzy with his drunken theatrics, feeding off our energy as he inched closer and closer to the edge. Everyone started to cheer. And finally, with the right jolt, he seized the legs and aired the thing over the edge, skidding and sliding over rocks and random brush for a respectable 15 yards.

Just before reaching terminal velocity, he lunged for a huge rock and grabbed onto the sucker to stop his slide—saving himself a trip to the hospital, or wherever it is that Reform Jews go when they slide down the mountain. But the Buffoon got his ride—and miraculously, he seemed unscathed as he bellowed something into the Haifa night, pounding his chest as he was set ablaze with adrenaline and glory. He shimmied down the slide to retrieve the near-ruined thing. And when he came back up to the flat nook of the party, he started whipping the crowd into a frenzy for another run.

As-Salibi and I both looked at Lee in disbelief. "Don't worry about them," said Lee. "They are, umm . . ." He searched for the English word. *"Crazy!"*

———

As the night progressed, As-Salibi and I started talking to more and more of the 30-something Israelis at the party. Like many Western Europeans, almost everyone in Israel speaks English. Even the Israelis who claim *not* to speak English will look you straight in the eye and say, "I'm sorry. I don't speak English." But everyone at this party was bilingual.

As I would soon find upon my arrival in Lebanon, most of the Israelis shared the great dream of *all* Mediterranean surfers to go to "a more serious place to surf." Like Hawaii. Or Australia. Or even that magical place in Baja my friend Kasey calls Lost Point.

After the surfing talk had subsided, I sat down on a horsehair blanket by the fire. Lee's uncle was picking out an Eric Clapton tune on a guitar and I was really feeling the groove, when I noticed As-Salibi on the far side of the party locked into race-car-paced blather with the Buffoon. I crept over to investigate.

"Dude," laughed the now inebriated As-Salibi when he saw me. "This guy says he was in Gaza a year ago." And in a deliberate stage whisper, he added, "Operation Cast Lead!"

"Yeahhh!!!" The Buffoon abruptly weighed in at a crowd-silencing decibel. "I was in Gaza. I *shoot* big gunnns and shhhit." The Buffoon was swaying in a solo sort of swagger. He didn't seem violent, just unpredictable.

As-Salibi, who worked for the Ma'an news agency, the most respected newswire in the Occupied Territories, then explained that a lot of strange, unconfirmed reports had been filed from Gaza during Operation Cast Lead. Invading units from Israel Defense Forces kicked Gazans out of their homes, using them as temporary bases, sleeping in their beds and eating their food. However, it was rumored that some units were ordered to take "extreme measures" to restore the condition of the homes during the month-long war. While it was never officially reported by the Ma'an news agency, some Gazans returned to their homes to find clean dishes and washed sheets. Others returned to human excrement smeared on their walls.

At the time of the Gaza War, As-Salibi had been too sick from the death count on the office white board to make any sense of this report. Besides, why would the Israelis blow the Gaza Strip to rubble, only to wash the sheets? It just didn't make sense. So As-Salibi just added it to the long list of unresolved reports from Gaza . . . but that was before he met the Buffoon.

As-Salibi leaned in close to me and said, "He was going off on how fucked the army was . . . he said it all depended on the commanders. He told me that some of them turned a blind eye, while others just sacked the place . . . and then I realized just what kind of unit he was in!"

"Yeah! Yeah! Can you beeelieve that shhhit?" cried the Buffoon, jumping in from out of nowhere. He shrieked, "I wasss a Gazaaa maid!"

BAHA'I VISA

Hey, I like your movies, man. You've got a great penis.

VAL KILMER as Jim Morrison in *The Doors*

The next thing I knew my head hurt and it was the morning after. The Haifa sun was blistering my skin and I was growing anxious because I had to be in Beirut in a week. I had enrolled in an Arabic program and knew it was going to be no cakewalk getting to that "hostile" Arab country from Israel—especially with Che tagging along as I went through Jerusalem, the West Bank, and Jordan and then landed at the Lebanese airport in Beirut.

My hangover had reduced my life's agenda to coffee and some quiet time with the newspaper at the Port Inn. But through an irrationally fierce campaign of coercion, As-Salibi had convinced me to cram myself into a taxi and head up the mountain for a tourist tour of the Baha'i Gardens. I was bitter. And now dehydrated.

The elderly European tourists had been comfortably sipping Beverage in their air-conditioned coaches all morning. But not us. I had sucked my plastic water bottle dry and there was going to be no refilling until our highly organized tour meandered its way to the bottom of this garden, planted on the face of the coastal escarpment.

Though it felt like an oven, the garden was beautiful. The immaculate levels of lush green grass were framed by exotic flowers in bright yellows and oranges. Some of the flowerbeds were positioned on the center of the grass, forming the nine-pointed star that symbolizes the Baha'i faith. At the bottom of the hill, over the tightly manicured levels, a giant orange dome sat, grounding the place with its bold exuberance. This tomb was the resting place of the Bab, the last messenger of the Baha'i faith.

The phrase "last messenger" is key. One of the sticking points in Islam—an Abrahamic religion—is that Mohammed was The Last Messenger from G-d, or Allah, or whatever. So it was a Serious Fucking Problem when the Ayatollah Khomeini overthrew the Shah of Iran in 1979 and deemed Baha'is to be "enemies of God" and subject to public execution. Needing to escape, the leaders of the Baha'i faith fled Iran and went to Cyprus, then Haifa, where the Bab's tomb dates from the 1890s. The Israeli government agreed to host this new "Mecca" of the Baha'i faith partly on the condition that Baha'is themselves would not *move* to Haifa, and thus not infringe on the Jewish character of the prestigious real estate. Yet it is the duty of every Baha'i to *visit*.

Our tour guide confirmed this when he sarcastically muttered through the midday heat, "It is the duty of all Baha'is to come spend money in Haifa as tourists."

As-Salibi grinned sheepishly.

Somebody from The Government clearly had had a chat with this boy, a convincing one.

But I was done playing tourist. I wanted to get moving to the West Bank. As-Salibi and I had planned to make our way to his Bethlehem flat and, like all travel in the Levant, it was going to be a time-consuming process. But there was As-Salibi, clicking his camera like some methadrine-fueled paparazzo, trying to capture The Perfect Shot of this Haifa paradise. I knew his manic-obsessive side well from Nablus, but this seemed different.

What was he not telling me?

Jesse: Salibi, you scurvy bastard! Why have you dragged me
            to this goddamn Baha'i garden in this goddamn heat?

As-Salibi: Ha! What?

Jesse: Why are we playing tourist with these goofy old timers?

As-Salibi: Dude, we gotta finish The Tour.

Jesse: Umm . . . why? Let's grab the bus to Jerusalem.

As-Salibi: Because I work at a Palestinian news agency and
            Israel doesn't view Ma'an as a "news organization."
            So, they won't give me a work permit here.

Jesse: What?

As-Salibi: Well, of course Ma'an is a news agency, the most
            respected in the Palestinian Territories. In one form
            or another, all Israelis read what we write, as it's
            quoted by Israeli papers. Even the *New York Times*.

Jesse: So what does this have to do with us and the Baha'i
            Gardens!?!

As-Salibi: To be a foreigner and work in Bethlehem as a jour-
            nalist, I have to come up with a reason for a visa—I
            can't keep renewing my tourist visa. Really, it comes
            down to one man: Daniel Seaman. A settler. Head
            of the Government Press Office. He and his junta
            decide who is eligible for a press card/work permit—
            they control everything!

(The Texan launched into his famously manic chuckle. And it was then I sensed something sly; a bamboozlement campaign was about to surface.)

As-Salibi: Well, according to my new visa, I am doing research
             on the Baha'i Gardens!

I enjoyed a dry-mouthed guffaw in the savage roast. The absurdity of As-Salibi's scam was just epic, and it was all the more amusing that now I could be deemed a "collaborator" in his stupid fucking scheme. A geeky grad student this dude was not!

As-Salibi went on. "And my plan is when the Israeli visa people 'check up' on me, I can email the Israel Ministry of Tourism my pictures and send them this report I typed up one night while drinking and scouring websites and stitching together a few facts."

My guffaw simmered into a smile of raw amusement. *Why not?* At the time, the Israeli government didn't issue visas for foreign journalists on the West Bank. There were no official channels. So a certain kind of cunning was needed to work on the West Bank, a place that may look like Israel on a map, but as As-Salibi—The Crusader—was starting to remind me, was a hell of a lot more complicated.

As the chief editor of the Ma'an news agency, Nasser Lahham, once said about Israel's journalist policy on the West Bank, "The Israelis don't care what is written about them in Arabic or in Hebrew, they only care about publications in English. Israel, especially after the war in Gaza, doesn't want certain things to be published and conveyed to English-speaking people in the world."

And that was it. To me, As-Salibi was the cowboy-journalist of the Orient, but on the job, this slick Texan was a respected journalist who reported the story of the Palestinian people . . . and in a language the world could understand.

I grew tense. Not because I faintly heard the Baha'i group leader chirp at us to keep up, but because reality had suddenly sunk in: we were on our way to the occupied West Bank.

Moving around the closed border—and surfing from Israel to Lebanon—was most definitely about to get underway. And the rules were about to change.

The gassing that ends every Friday protest in the West Bank village of Bil'in

SECOND LEG

UP, BUT FIRST AROUND:
ISRAEL TO LEBANON

All distances in the East are measured by hours, not miles. A good horse will walk three miles an hour over nearly any kind of a road; therefore, an hour, here, always stands for three miles. This method of computation is bothersome and annoying; and until one gets thoroughly accustomed to it, it carries no intelligence to his mind until he has stopped and translated the pagan hours into Christian miles, just as people do with the spoken words of a foreign language they are acquainted with, but not familiarly enough to catch the meaning in a moment.

MARK TWAIN, *The Innocents Abroad*

JERUSALEM, YERUSHALAYIM, AL-QUDS

*Jerusalem Syndrome is actually a rare psychological con-
dition that occurs to some visitors to the Middle East.
They get to Israel and just snap.*

MARC MARON

Traditionally, empires ruled the Middle East. They would rise like a wave from the depths, building to a crest so powerful its explosion would take everything that lay in its path. But like all waves, these empires eventually rolled back, leaving only a wet shore as proof of their past existence. And that is Jerusalem—a withered maze of ancient empires, built literally atop one another.

If Haifa was the city of Arabs and Jews, then Jerusalem was the reef that caused it all to break. Yet Jerusalem would be a detour for me—the place I'd go because I couldn't cross the closed Israeli-Lebanese border to Beirut, not more than twenty miles from the Haifa surf crew. And so the Holy City became a strange sort of portal for me: the place from which I would leave Jewish culture and take my first steps into the Arab world. No fine lines of transition, just crossing—with all the history and myth that make Jerusalem the prized shore of nearly every cresting empire . . . and the best medieval costume party on earth.

And so, it was time to get grounded. Time to give Lee one last call and email my editor at the *Surfer's Journal* to say I had just scored some waves in Israel and was now on my way to Lebanon with the story. It was time to round up Che and As-Salibi, and time check out of the Port Inn and head to the Haifa train station. It was time to do the job.

When we arrived at the Haifa bus station there was the standard shakedown of Israeli security, but everything fell easily into place. I slid Che effortlessly into the bottom of the bus then climbed the stairs only to see row upon row of Religious Jews . . . in nearly every seat. I remember thinking something like, *Holy Dreadlocked Moses! Surfing was never taught in this Hebrew school. What kind of sick joke was this, taking a surfboard to Jerusalem?*

Gliding through the ancient hills along the open Israeli roads, I started thinking that to the Jew, this city is *Yerushalayim*. To the Christian, this city is Jerusalem. To the Muslim, this city is *al-Quds*. But for As-Salibi and me, this city was lunch.

We weren't exactly on some theological crusade. The only mystical experience we were looking for was to sink our fangs into some kind of devilish street schnitzel. And when we got to Jerusalem, it was everywhere. Just a good stumble outside the bus station we found shops and stands filled with its greasy goodness.

"Maybe we should take a cab," I muttered, between gnawing at the schnitzel.

"Nah," As-Salibi countered, also gnawing. "Jaffa Street is pretty cool. With your surfboard, it will take just as long to find a taxi as walk."

So we decided to walk Jaffa Street, the historical no-man's-land that once nominally split the difference between East and

West Jerusalem. This was the 1949 Armistice Line, all right. The Green Line. The same road that was once covered with heavy barbed wire, fortified with snipers and hunkered-down military units on all sides. Then, in 1967, when the Israelis captured East Jerusalem in the Six-Day War, Jaffa Street was cleared and brought under the blue and white of the Israeli flag. But even with the Israeli victory and the clearing of Jaffa Street, it was still a mission to negotiate a six-foot surfboard through the hurried people, blow-by buses, and jammed sidewalks.

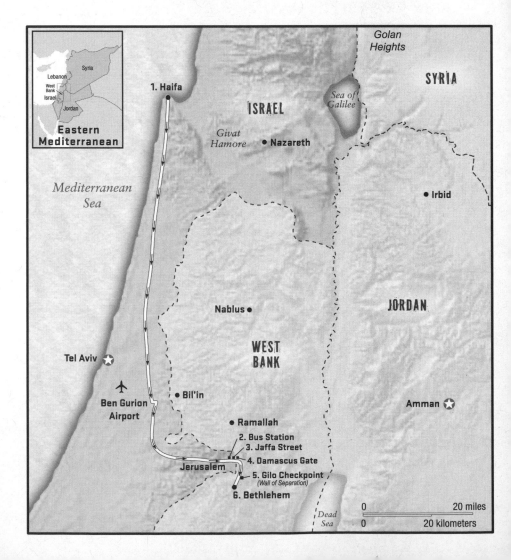

In all its history, there has never been a reason to bring a surfboard to Jaffa Street. There is no surf. Jerusalem is a land-locked Religious city on a hill. But our objective wasn't the physical dance of wave riding. Jaffa Street was simply a hub that would connect me to Lebanon, as there could be no direct meandering up the coast from Haifa. The closed border was in the way, with both Israel and Hezbollah taking the fiercest aim at one another. The only way to surf up the Eastern Mediterranean coast would be this little experiment: come back down to Jerusalem, cross the West Bank into Jordan, fly over Syria, and land at the Beirut airport in Lebanon. It was going to require two American pass-ports—as the Lebanese gleefully deny entry to any and all saps foolish enough to enter with a stamp on their passport from Israel . . . a country they're still technically at war with. So there I was, walking on Jaffa Street, just passing on through to Lebanon, with perhaps the only reason anyone would ever bring a surfboard to this landlocked, Biblical city on a hill.

I felt like some kind of Roman with a klutzy surfboard *pilum*, holding Che high by his shoulder strap as we stumbled through the streets together. Orthodox and Ultra-Orthodox Jews frantically tried to pass as I worked to negotiate Che around old street posts; new street posts; and even a pay phone, hidden under a collage of Hebrew letters. It was madness in all direc-tions. Everywhere I looked there were people. A sudden blast from a passing bus blew Che wildly, like a half-opened parachute. Once, I nearly harpooned an old babushka with Slavic features. *Was she Russian Jewish?* This was rush hour on Jaffa Street. A new kind of ride with my board that even my wildest fantasies hadn't quite captured.

The further As-Salibi and I wandered, the more cosmopolitan Jaffa Street became, with outdoor coffee shops and cafés, stone neighborhoods, and overpriced trinket shops with polished old things I didn't need. At some undefined point, the crowd made a philosophical—almost historical—shift from Orthodox to a Reform brand of liberal Judaism. And then, it shifted back.

I suddenly remembered an Irish barfly I briefly met in Tel Aviv a few years before, who said, "Visit Jerusalem. I'm not even a religious person but it made the hair on my arms stick up. You'll know when you're there it's a religious city." And sweet Jesus, the mick fool was right! Jaffa is a far cry from the hedonistic streets of Tel Aviv, but just because everyone is more traditional doesn't take the fun out of the place. The religious costume party is not only enjoyable to watch but has an amazing ability to make you feel hip, normal, and thankful to your parents for not rejecting the past thousand years of human evolution when they raised you. Then there are those who claim to feel that special spiritual something in the Holy City . . . but there's not enough bourbon on my desk as I write here in Santa Barbara to get tangled with that.

Though it strives to be, Jerusalem can never be an everyday city. Too many people examine this place from afar, like scientists peering off with wonder at some wonderfully lit planet too far from reach. When foreigners first visit Jerusalem, they tend to lay their own fantasies on the place, as many of them have spent a lifetime singing and praying and philosophizing about it. But what does it matter? It's holy for them, too. Even if only in a cultural sense. Which is a major reason Jerusalem has so many names. It's important to more people than could possibly be known. In all kinds of ways.

Somewhere around this point of pondering the meaning of it all, there tends to be a dip southward as the mind echoes the same sort of passiveness that can be found in the residents of Jaffa Street. *Who the fuck cares what everyone else thinks?* When you've spent enough time in a holy place, the *so-called* holiness of it kills off whatever mystique *actually* inhabits it. But I had just gotten to Jaffa Street . . . so my dispassion was from that bulky fiberglass bastard, Che, making my shoulders numb as I kept passing him off from one side to the other. And I could tell that it was the tourists—*not* the costume-party locals—who were looking at me in amazement. *Perhaps a Californian with his surfboard wasn't the idol they expected to see in the city that grounded their faith.* Che and I smiled in amusement.

As we continued down Jaffa, As-Salibi was out in front and I paused for another much needed moment of calm. It was imperative that I regroup. Sometimes when traveling, things get so massively overwhelming that it is in the interest of your own safety that you take a break before the scene gets too frightening. While you expect a certain payoff of personal growth from lunging yourself into unforeseen situations, there is always the risk of getting bucked off the wagon. And that can be a very bad thing. Especially in a place that is beyond your control, with people rushing by, while you are lugging a bag, handling a goddamn surfboard, and trying to inhale as much culture as can be safely whiffed.

Holding this pause, I looked down to see that the hairs on my arms were on end—just as the mick fool had predicted! Continuing to tune out, I let my mind wander off to some half-naked Catholic/pagan kid halfway around the world in Peru, on a high plane in the Andes Mountains, dreaming off into the distance about the historic spot where Jesus was crucified. *Not too far from where I'm standing.* A mean sense of awe started to sneak up on me . . . the Church of the Holy Sepulchre. And every step I took down Jaffa Street would lead me closer to the crucifixion site in the Old City. I shuddered with a blast of Jerusalem Syndrome, took a deep breath, forced myself to stop thinking about it, and moved on.

Then I came around a small shelter. It was a bus waiting zone with Hebrew letters smothered all over it like the pay phone a few blocks back. I couldn't understand the words, and the bulky steel of the foundation forced me to swing Che wide behind it, near the guardrail, and onto the steps of a shoemaker's storefront. There, I saw a lone Hassid. Suddenly, in the familiar drawl of California English, he spoke. "Hey! Whatcha got in the bag?"

I looked him over. The man was nearly identical to every other Hassid I had seen: black straight-brimmed hat, white collared shirt with the top button rigidly fastened, black belt, black trousers, black shoes—and a very nice black beard, which really tied it all together.

"Oh, hey. What's up, dude?" I replied, in that same brand of California speech. "Umm . . . it's a surfboard!"

"A surfboard!? In Jerusalem? *Why?*"

"I'm doing a story for a surfing magazine. I was just surfing near Haifa."

Utter amazement took over. "Wow! I had no idea." Then bewilderment took hold and words escaped him.

"Yeah . . ." I started back in. "It was actually quite—"

"See," the Hassid burst out, "I'm from Long Beach, California. I surfed in L.A. once, but I had no idea you could surf in Israel!"

Every piece of self-restraint I had was now geared toward *not* picturing this Hassidic museum piece trying to surf off the coast of Los Angeles in the sea of fake tits and beach culture.

"Do people actually surf here?" he asked. "Well, if they do, I've got to get to Tel Aviv and try it . . ." Muttering something about a surfboard, the Hassid ran his fingers through his long, black beard, then swiveled and disappeared into the shoemaker's shop. He was gone as suddenly as he had appeared.

Jerusalem. It was most definitely a trip.

———

When a foreigner walks through Jerusalem, the biggest impression often comes at the end of Jaffa Street. It's where an abrupt left turn is made, and where the parapets of the Old City come into focus. The gradual downhill slope, next to the grassy lawn, makes for an easy finish at the Damascus Gate. The Ottoman walls of the Old City are most amazing here. The sand-colored stones gleam high in the sunlight and the jagged edges hint back to an earlier time for humanity, when you actually had to layer your defenses so that deviants with arrows could shoot at whatever infidel seemed to be invading. Now, everyone has fighter jets and whatever the hell Saddam used, and thus the gradual decline from Jaffa Street to the Damascus Gate is now better known for great pictures, the entrance to the Old City, and the best place to catch a taxi to Bethlehem.

Then a strange feeling crept into the air—like something had changed and we missed it. *Had As-Salibi, Che, and I missed it? No . . . we couldn't have.* Waving Che back through the air, I turned around, only to find *Palestinians*. Everywhere. Speaking Arabic! I had taken my first steps into the Arab world and hadn't even realized it. *Where on Jaffa Street did it change? After the Hassid?*

The air no longer smelled of European cuisine and watered-down Western coffee but of juicy kabobs, roasting in the open air on robust street grills. The scent of giant pans of cheese-filled *kunafa* and other tempting Arab pastries wafted unapologetically up my nostrils. Arab merchants were all around me, selling sneakers, dress pants, and flimsy plastic toys assembled with an already-broken Chinese charm.

"It's like we just walked into a whole new country," I said to As-Salibi, exhaling in amazement. He was standing next to me and I handed Che to him for a moment's relief. The Texan smiled. Few hour-long stumbles in this world can provide such an education.

———

Standing there, looking vaguely back up the way, the bits I remembered about Jaffa Street's history came twisting back into focus. From 1949 to 1967 it was the fortified divide between East and West Jerusalem, the forbidden entrance to the inland Arabdom from the young Jewish state. Ever since Israel won the 1967 War and united Jaffa Street under the Israeli flag, Jewish businesses have moved in, making the road seem less grim than what the old black-and-white pictures of machine guns and barbed wire seemed to suggest.

So with all this history simmering on Jaffa Street, it takes a particular kind of nerve *not* to enjoy the safety of the free transportation along the open roadway. You need a reason to justify walking from the bus station to the Old City. It's all open now. And thanks to As-Salibi's urging, we carried Che and our bags through the old roadblocks of history and experienced firsthand how Jaffa Street can still be a most interesting place to walk.

I took my first steps into the Arab world and I didn't even know it.

MOTHER, SHOULD I BUILD A WALL?

*Sometimes I wonder whether the world is being run
by smart people who are putting us on, or by imbeciles
who really mean it.*

MARK TWAIN

In front of the Damascus Gate, there is always a packed line of
cab-driving Palestinians violently huffing cigarettes. Even if it's
just for a moment, it's imperative to talk to them, as you are doing
everyone a favor by disrupting their chain-smoking vice. Without
pause, As-Salibi started a conversation with some Arabic phrase
I didn't understand. Holding Che upright, he was coming off like
some Persian peacock, giving the illusion of size. It was clear he
was locked in brutal and occasionally harsh negotiations, though
I knew it was just cabbie dialect: "How much to the Wall?" I took
a step back.

Everything was negotiated individually—Che, what supplies were needed to tie Che to the roof, As-Salibi's bag, my bag,
As-Salibi's friend; and I was later told that engine oil was also
brought up. As-Salibi was a master of the art: wave your arms
with a hint of Fucking Madman Hysteria, and the price always
goes down.

"Settled!" As-Salibi suddenly cried, with euphoria now in
the air.

Everyone shook hands and patted each other on the back
as if some non-inevitable deal had been miraculously hammered
into a solid accord. Done. Time for another smoke.

For my part, I snapped a few stealthy pictures as four Arab men in gray slacks shifted the conversation to a public debate on the best way to tie a surfboard to the roof. Done. One last smoke, then off to the West Bank and The Wall that divides it from Israel proper.

———

The mainstream press no longer bothers to write about the existence of the Jewish state and Jews' right to cross the 1967 Jaffa Street divide to visit the Western Wall. That has been settled. Rather, journalists write about the towering monstrosity that hugs the hilltops of Judea and Samaria, dividing Israel proper from the West Bank. Thus, for all intents and purposes, Israel's "wall of separation" is now, officially, The Wall. It's the only one making news anymore.

And then, we approached it. Giving our Palestinian cabbie a damn-near heart attack as we moved closer to the occupation and the West Bank, I stuck my head out the window, aiming the ten-megapixel Canon camera my mom bought me, to capture the gray blandness of its divisive "Fuck you."

Just as we were literally about to hit the thing, the cabbie broke hard and twisted in his seat, making a tight U-turn that didn't let up until his cab was pointed all the way back toward Jerusalem. Everything in his body seemed to want to be away from The Wall, the warehouse-like checkpoint, and the concrete cage where many of his Palestinian brethren were kept.

Already things seemed different. No more cosmopolitan Jerusalem Jews. Only green-uniformed Israeli soldiers, settlers passing to Rachel's Tomb, and a sea of pants-and-collar Palestinian men smoking in front of the warehouse checkpoint of The Wall.

As-Salibi and I got out, paid the cabbie, and unstrapped Che. As-Salibi said a few unimportant things to the cabbie, as I hoisted Che onto my shoulder and started into the grayish building, the portal to the West Bank: the Israeli checkpoint.

Inside the warehouse checkpoint was a grocery store–like checkout line of multiple bulletproof cases containing Israeli soldiers. The tension was most definitely lurking.

"The Israelis almost never ask why you're coming *into* the West Bank," As-Salibi said. "But if they do, you're fucking *not with me*."

I laughed.

"Just pretend you're some fanatical Christian who wants to get closer to Jesus or something. They get a lot of *that* around here."

About 15 feet above us, I noticed a metal pathway, suspended in the air, connecting the warehouse. Still looking up, I saw what looked like a Moroccan Jew, glaring at me. He was sporting a yarmulke with a blue Israeli flag, a T-shirt, desert cargo pants, and an assault rifle; the black paint was worn down to the metal where he had been gripping it tightly. He was antsy, clutching the firearm as if he might have to sprint to the other side of the checkpoint—without warning—and spray a suicide bomber full of lead. This dude was *not* a surfer.

I could tell that he was a serious guy, all right, but also just another 20-something of the world whose main priorities were getting drunk and getting laid. Kind of like, well, me. And I had no doubt that I could do a few shots with the kid in the context of some crude bar, but he was on guard here—and

I knew he wouldn't hesitate to shoot me for things that in my world were filed strictly under Savage Humor. I was tempted to poke, but some rudimentary element of survival kicked in, and I thought it would be better to just pass through. Away from The Edge.

——————

When we reached the first gate of the checkpoint, I had to swing Che wide and go in backward. It was the only way to get through, because the rotisserie gates were set up for one-way traffic into Jerusalem. I couldn't tell if the Israelis were trying to make things difficult or if the arrangement just reflected their thinking: *who the hell would want to go into the West Bank?*

At the entry of the thing was a cute Israeli teen with curly black hair sitting in a bulletproof booth. Her green army uniform was noticeably unbuttoned down the top and I crept up on my tiptoes to investigate her tight and inviting breasts. She smiled. I smiled back. I looked straight into her eyes. She giggled, lifted her finger, pointed, and said "Pass!" And she didn't stop giggling as I left.

As-Salibi, Che, and I strolled out of the warehouse checkpoint and into a strangely vacant lot with massive lights shining down on us. We couldn't see who was watching. And it felt strange being locked somewhere between the security layers of The Wall. It wasn't quite the West Bank, and we definitely weren't on the outskirts of Jerusalem anymore.

"Dude, they didn't even ask a question," I half-whispered to Salibi.

"Well, don't get too comfortable," As-Salibi scolded. "See those cameras? They are watching us . . . right now. Keep walking. No looking around."

Across the lot I could see another rotisserie cattle guard standing uninhabited in the cool night. I knew this was the final one that opened into the West Bank. I felt a tremor of anxiety but kept thinking, *No. Going. Back.*

Approaching the gate, we came around to an adjacent bulletproof case with another cute Israeli teenage girl sitting inside. We needed her to press the little red button inside her booth so that the green button on top of the gate would open this final barrier to the West Bank.

The closer we got, the more it became clear that she was actually asleep. Her legs were slightly raised in the air and her hand was bracing her blushing cheek to keep her head resting in a light sleep. From the look on her face, I playfully imagined she was dreaming of a reassignment from army duty, maybe on a Birthright Israel trip where some kosher American dude would take her away on a wild caravan as far from the Israeli occupation as possible.

Before I met up with the Haifa surfers, that dude could have been, well, me. (That's right, I had gotten to the Middle East on a fully subsidized Birthright Israel trip to get in touch with my "Jewish roots." But that was already a lifetime ago and the cool Californian in me that might try to whisk her away was literally about to cross the The Wall to the West Bank.)

I calmly said a few things at the opening of her bulletproof glass case, trying to wake her, but failed.

"Ahh, shit," I said, pulling back. "What now?"

As-Salibi shrugged and laughed nervously. "Umm, wake her up?"

The air was still and the sounds of the night were calm to the point that I didn't want to disturb it. There were no soldiers around, and it seemed like nobody had gone through in a good long while. So I reached out and mustered the most nonthreatening fist I could and knocked hard on the glass.

"Hello? Shalom. Are you there?"

Silence.

The glass was too thick. I tightened my fist a hair and raised my voice a decibel. "Hello!?"

Suddenly, the girl jolted. She looked stunned, with a little guilt, as if the Birthright magic I'd imagined for her had been busted in upon in the rudest way. Regaining her composure, she quickly adjusted her beret, brushed her chest in a jerk and looked at us with embarrassed bewilderment. She leaned forward, her lips softly approaching the microphone and started with a seductively self-conscious accent.

"Hello? Hi. Where are you from?"

"Oh, hey. I'm from California—you know . . . umm . . . California?"

A few years ago in the West Bank I learned that the more I could come off like a jackoff from California, the more I could break through the stiffness of Israeli security. Turns out that most Israelis loathe keeping up the persecutor mentality of the West Bank, as it often reminds them of something else. To get away from it, they love to hang out with foreigners—especially those from the Jewish Diaspora.

So I did my best to accommodate, trying to sound like some

"Chad from Malibu" surf character who didn't understand why the hell she was sitting in a bulletproof box in front of The Wall that divides Israel proper from the West Bank. And it worked.

"*Ohh*, California . . ."

"Yeah, California . . . umm . . . ever been?"

"*No*. But someday . . . after the army." She pointed. "What is that?"

"California?"

"Lo!" (*Lo* is the Hebrew word for "no.") She giggled. "That!" Laughing now, she pointed at Che in his bag.

"Oh, that!" I shrugged and laughed, working the delight-fully sheepish angle. "A surfboard."

She slid off her stool in a youthful way that we recognized. Leaning up to the bulletproof glass, she took a quick glance at Che, and then plopped back onto her seat.

By this point, As-Salibi, Che, and I were doing everything we could to keep from laughing. This chick couldn't have been older than we were, and while she seemed girly and harmless, she held our fate in her hands. You can never underestimate the power that the state of Israel bestows on seemingly harmless Jewesses. A cultural difference indeed, especially when compared to the Palestinians, who lived just beyond the turn of her gate. A red flag here could mean a lot of uncomfortable questions for us, like, "Why the fuck are you bringing a surfboard to the West Bank?" So to keep things from getting too surreal, Che, As-Salibi, and I resorted to imagining her in the nude with a machine gun. Why not?

Eventually, the girl let us go through, and giggled as she watched As-Salibi and me try to cram Che sideways through her unforgiving metal rotisserie gate to the West Bank.

It crossed my mind to yell back through the gate for her number. But I didn't. We were already walking through the chain-link tunnel that ran next to The Wall and had entered a strange new world, a few centuries older looking than Israel on the "other side."

Through the fence ahead, I could make out mounds of old scrap and half-abandoned buildings. A chorus of goddamn hounds was barking in a rabid chaos, piercing the calm night air in a way that couldn't be heard on the other side of the concrete Wall. The lack of light and the medieval colors made it feel like entering the lion's cage. The vibe in the air was of reckless and random danger. These gutted, neglected buildings advertised an angry warning, "Do Not Enter," which could shake even the most loyal Palestinian supporter.

If I ever held any doubts about going back to the West Bank after my experience in Nablus, they were gone. Because this whole thing really wasn't about caging off territory or stopping suicide bombers or securing land in a future two-state agreement. It's plain old psychology, an edict from the Israeli government to Palestinians designed to make them feel like an unwelcomed, defeated people.

Every step in that chain-link tunnel was like moving a notch forward, squeezing my sensory glands in a vice. And all I wanted to do was return to the fine bosom of five minutes ago. But there was no going back. Decisions had been made. And I had to stick to them, hoping to live long enough to collect the eventual pay-off I'd gain from leaving The Comfortable. Whatever happened, the prize was the same as in any adventure: pushing the limits of the journey and the beast in yourself.

Though we were nominally safe behind our American pass-ports and bumbling "duder" personas, suppressing our internal flashing warning lights was not an easy thing. Che, As-Salibi, and I continued moving steadily through the tunnel, past the famous "Jesus wept for Jerusalem" graffiti, to the eventual mob of make-shift cab drivers, yelling frantically in English, "Go where?!"

Fucking Kansas was in the tornado, twisting up into the ether.

BETHLEHEM PORCH

*In guerrilla terminology, strategy is understood as the
analysis of the objectives to be achieved in the light
of the total military situation and the overall ways of
reaching these objectives.*

CHE GUEVARA, *Guerrilla Warfare*

The West Bank is marvelous terrain for the guerrilla. Its rolling
hills, covered with washed slabs of white rock, make for easy
hiding from everything conventional. Israel's famed Merkava
tanks (literally "God's Chariots") feel the burden of the ground
here. These are not the baking sands of the Sinai Desert they
were designed for. Then there is the human element of the West
Bank. Everyone knows everyone, and the civilian population has
hardened generations to combat all things Israeli; their collective
intelligence has been honed for this sole purpose. Even some of
the apartment buildings on the West Bank—many designed by
local architects—look as if they were built to deter Israeli raids:
they reflect the white rock of the hills and are huddled inward in
a way that would make any convoy commander wary of snipers
and RPG fire from higher ground.

But the West Bank is mostly calm these days. There are
no more intifadas, no suicide bombings, and no warfare raging
through the streets. Since the last time I was in the West Bank,
in 2007, the Palestinian Authority had brought an assortment of
former militiamen under their official banner. In all honesty, the
Palestinian Authority is more afraid of the Islamic Resistance

Movement (Hamas) than it is afraid of the Israelis.

So it was a surprise when, after only an hour in the West Bank—just as we got to As-Salibi's apartment—we heard gunshots echo through the walls.

Reacting quickly, I switched my camera to video and held it at arm's length, pointing it toward me. "I just got to the West Bank. I've been here for about an hour. I'm eating *shawarma* with As-Salibi in his high-rise apartment in Bethlehem. And, ahh . . . bullets and shots are being shot from over there . . . There's a refugee camp. You have a comment, Salib?"

"Welcome home."

"Jesus, man!" I said to As-Salibi, shaking my head and setting the camera down.

"Never mind," he snapped. "That stuff *rarely* happens here. Not in Bethlehem, for God's sake! Totally rare, what we heard tonight. Take a seat, man. Have a beer."

As we sat on As-Salibi's porch, I started to take in what the architects had done. The more I looked at it, the more I could see that the seven-building apartment complex seemed guilty of being huddled in a circle of protection. Every window had an outside cast-iron cage bolted onto it. Every porch was encased with tall, thick stone. Every kitchen had an awkward, small window for the quick peep outside. *Christ, the place looked ready to resist a Soviet invasion!*

In the middle of these large white buildings was a rundown park with a swing-less swing set and a leaning streetlight that painted everything with a strange yellow ambiance, as if we were on the ruined set of some action-packed Oriental Blockbuster.

After my wandering eyes took focus, the calm of the clear Bethlehem night set in. There was a strange feeling of peace, as if the gunshots were an entire five minutes ago. In the lull, As-Salibi and I started vocalizing again.

Jesse: So, Salib, you're the only gringo in this apartment complex?

As-Salibi: Yeah, man. It's crazy. I mean, it's cool, but crazy. I really like my neighbors and they are very protective of me. I couldn't feel safer, really . . . some are like family.

Jesse: Yeah?

As-Salibi: Even my landlord is cool. It's great: we have no lease, no piece of paper that says how much I owe him a month . . . or even that I live here! But if he were to mess with me—or the other way around—he couldn't because it would harm our *reputations*.

Jesse: Your reputations?

As-Salibi: See, everyone knows everyone here. You don't just casually move around. So people get "reputations." If he were to mess with me, he'd have to deal with everyone in this building and everyone at my job; the same is true for me.

It was an interesting concept. Something that sounded familiar from my prior experience in Lebanon and the West Bank. In contrast to the institution-crazed mindset of go-fuck-yourself America, everything works through personal relationships and local channels of communication in the Middle East. And it definitely holds true for the Palestinians in the West Bank. A notable cross-cultural difference, indeed.

As-Salibi: Actually, funny story: so like the only rule my land-lord made with me—besides *not* collaborating with the Israelis (laughs)—was that I had to be careful who I brought over.

Jesse: Yeah? (I nodded, shrugging somewhat indifferently as my eyes went back on the yellow-lit building across the way.)

As-Salibi: See, there is this Palestinian girl who works at Ma'an, and we were working on a project together. She's a Christian. From Bethlehem. And I forgot something in my apartment for this project we were working on together, like a paper or something, I can't even remember. Anyway, she comes over after work . . . and I'm not about to leave her on the street, right? So she comes up for literally 30 seconds. Literally!

Jesse: Literally!?

As-Salibi: Literally! And the next day I get this phone call from my landlord saying he's on his way over. He gets here, takes a seat on the couch, lights a ciga-rette, and says, "Look Salibi, I'm a Marxist . . . I care about *nothing*. Do whatever you want. Really. Anything at all. It won't be a problem. But you can't bring Palestinian girls up here. See, people talk. And I cannot have some blood feud with her brother or something."

Jesse: Well, Jesus, Salibi, you crusader! Taking their women!?

As-Salibi: Just for 30 seconds, man! Can you believe it!? So you need to be careful with things like that around here. It's part of the whole conservative Arab thing.

As-Salibi was amused by the absurdity. He let out a chuckle, but not the standard manic West Bank giggles I remembered from Nablus.

The air fell quiet again on his Bethlehem porch and As-Salibi slouched down in a plastic chair. Then there was a moment we gazed through the clear night air, again onto the buildings' Blockbuster glow across the way.

As-Salibi slightly broke the calm by muttering something about how his landlord bought this unit because you couldn't see Har Homa, the Israeli settlement mostly behind the apartment building we were loosely staring at.

And then, suddenly, the madman jumped upright in his seat. Pounding his feet on the porch, he repeated: "Look, I'm a Marxist, I care about nothing! Ha! That's how my landlord started the whole conversation!"

The Texan was back, lit with his manic West Bank laughter.

ALLAH'S WORD

Young men who like their comforts and a dainty table,
or who wish to pass their time pleasantly in the com-
pany of women, must not go to Arabia.

CARSTEN NIEBUHR, *Description of Arabia*, 1774

On a dusty old cot in As-Salibi's apartment, with my eyes closed, I found myself somewhere between animist Dreamtime and the supposed conscious realm. I was resting. Out in the living room was Che, my foamy travel companion—my catalyst for meeting people, defusing tensions, and telling my story. My purpose. My reason. My vessel for the ride. But in that half-sleeping state, it all seemed so flimsy. A surfboard in the Middle East? How was that a reason?

Sure, I'd found an editor who liked the idea of surfing in the Middle East, but for all I knew surfing from Israel to Lebanon might not even be possible. What if it wasn't? Or what if I managed to figure out a way to do it, but the editor rejected my story? Where would I be then? This could be my most brutal failure. At age 24. "Stranded on the West Bank with a Surfboard." Jesus, what a fucking headline that would be. But really, surfing from Israel to Lebanon . . . was that just a wild, late-night mirage that had somehow hardened into reality? Or was I safely in bed in Santa Barbara, about to open my eyes to another fine California day?

Then I heard it: the literal word of God—that phantasmal expression of Arabian monotheism—wandered in through the window. I rolled over on my saggy cot. It was the Friday prayer, all right. On this day the muezzin's call to prayer was not just the *Shahada*, or testament of faith, but a verse from the Holy Koran (the literal word of God) that Allah had revealed by way of the Archangel Gabriel to the Prophet Mohammed in seventh-century Arabia. Its poetic tunes hint at a sort of holy methodology for remembering things. It's the sign of a culture with a strong oral tradition, where the memory is aided by the poetic tones of the voice. Which reminded me of how I learned my ABCs as a child with dyslexia. If you can't rely on reading the letters, enrich them, add another dimension, remember the harmony of their sounds . . . and thou *shall* remember.

Suddenly, another sound entered the airwaves.

Hhhheeik! Hhhheeik!

What was that!? Had my mind been abducted by last night's journey? Jesus, was I even awake?

"Ahh, shit! You hear that!?" As-Salibi came crashing out of his bed in a bumbling post-dawn chaos. "Jess, quick!" cried the half-naked As-Salibi, leaning over my face with his electrified Einstein hairdo. "Do you have any shekels?"

Creeping Jesus, I was definitely awake! Nobody asks me for Israeli money in my dreams.

"Umm, sure," I groaned with annoyance, rolling over on the old cot and throwing some coins at The Crusader Bastard. I laboriously sat upright on the old West Bank cot, cursing. I steadied my hands on my head to quell my throbbing under-slept dizziness. Everything seemed unstable.

I heard the iron door of As-Salibi's apartment crash closed.

Two minutes later, it crashed again. And when he came in, I was still struggling.

"Get up!" As-Salibi chirped, with the muezzin's call still singing in the airwaves. "I'll make coffee and you can start on The Bread."

I moaned like a beaten Bethlehem mutt. "The Bread?"

"The Bread!" re-chirped As-Salibi, now feeling a rush of adrenaline I could not find. "That *hhhheeik* sound is from this guy who comes around in the morning with fresh bread."

Forcing myself off the cot, I noticed a seemingly ancient dust trail following me . . . though I somewhat escaped it as I stumbled into the kitchen. I took a seat in an old wooden chair and started to nibble on a soft corner of the tender bread. It was indeed fresh—full of goodness and that soft, spongy quality that confirmed it was baked by some poor soul who had awakened even earlier than we had.

Loitering next to his brown kitten stove, As-Salibi was getting antsy, occasionally stirring the bubbling brew of roasting Arabic coffee. And then, the prayers stopped. Allah's word was finished. Since I had first opened my eyes—a whole 15 minutes ago—the morning prayers had been soaring out from a nearby mosque, broadcast through an elaborate set of minaret speakers and into As-Salibi's Bethlehem apartment. And now, utter silence. Nothingness. Not even a bark from those damned Bethlehem hounds.

I sat there, pondering, slowing working The Bread. Across the room, Che had no remark, as he nestled next to As-Salibi's Christmas tree. *Either it was always Christmas in Bethlehem or Salibi was just one lazy—*

As-Salibi broke in: "It's so fitting they have extended prayer on Friday, The Day of Protest . . ."

I dry-gulped the bread.

The Day of Protest!?

THE BATTLE OF BIL'IN

Hebrew and Arabic are closer to each other than to any third tongue. The Arabic greeting salaam aleikum *("peace be upon you") is* shalom aleikum *in Hebrew, though it's not a phrase often spoken between Arab and Jew.*

TONY HORWITZ, *Baghdad Without a Map and Other Misadventures in Arabia*

Just before I arrived in Haifa, when I was on that Birthright Israel trip, I had a chance to interview a former Israeli commando. "If Israel wants peace," I asked, "why does it continually violate the Green Line with The Wall? Isn't a secure Israeli state along the '67 lines a good deal . . . I mean, for Israel?"

"Good question," said the former commando, who had put his life on the line for his Jewish state. He too seemed to think that giving the West Bank, Gaza, and East Jerusalem to moderate Palestinians would be a pretty sweet gig for the future of Israeli security. And that way of thinking is more common among Israelis than you might expect.

But if you look at a map, the tragedy of the small village of Bil'in is immediately clear: it is 2.5 miles east of the 1949 Green Line—the same line Che, As-Salibi, and I had crossed on Jaffa Street in Jerusalem a few days before. Simply put, it is too close to Jerusalem, Tel Aviv, and Ben Gurion Airport. A rocket attack from the sleepy hills of Bil'in would shut down the Israeli economy, prompting a reinvasion of the West Bank, making Ariel Sharon's 2002 operation look like a goddamn kindergarten.

To avoid that scene, the Israelis moved The Wall across the

Green Line, breaching the 1967 border agreement, and annexed over 50 percent of the farmland of Bil'in. Further enraging the people of Bil'in, Israel erected one of those West Bank settlements there, sending a message that they would never get their farmland back, as it was now a buffer for Israeli state security.

From the outside, it might have seemed like violence would be the natural next move for the Palestinians. But it wasn't. The people of Bil'in moved away from the "intifada model" of resistance and did something even more radical: they filed a petition in Israel's Supreme Court. Now, keep in mind that this court hasn't exactly held a reputation for siding with Palestinian rights. But sweet Jesus, the villagers won! In a 2007 landmark verdict against the Israeli Army, the Supreme Court ordered that some of the farmland be returned. But then the Israeli Army did nothing. They ignored the Supreme Court's ruling, keeping The Wall—which in this section was only a set of chain-link fences—in the same place. To protest, the villagers started demonstrating, falling into a regular Day of Protest. Friday. Just after the local muezzin finished his extended noontime prayers.

From the other side of the fence—from the Israeli perspective—securing places along the Green Line was nothing cerebral; it was just the bitter brass tacks of "Israeli security." And there can be no compromise for any country when it comes to their security . . . or at least a perceived version of it. For the Israelis, why should Bil'in have been any different?

This was the situation. And it erupted every Friday like clockwork. Where villagers—accompanied by activists and journalists—marched to The Wall to meet the Israeli Army. On both sides, ready to go, only a chain-link fence between them.

As for As-Salibi and Jared (As-Salibi's boss at the Ma'an news agency), well, they just fucking lived for this stuff. On The Day of Protest, they would want to be nowhere else but the front line, snapping pictures, making sure that whatever happened would be meticulously documented, whatever the cost.

And so the three of us gathered near As-Salibi's apartment in Bethlehem that Friday, just outside what the boys jokingly called The Hamas Shop, for a chat and some supplies. Then it was off to the races. It was the day when Bil'in and a few other small Palestinian villages—which the Western world would never hear or care about otherwise—demonstrated against The Wall, the crossing of the Green Line, and the taking of farmland they needed to survive.

As-Salibi and I loitered outside while Jared went inside to negotiate some water and cigarettes. The Hamas Shop was the only store open in Bethlehem at that hour. It was run by two black-bearded brothers, very Islamic dudes who had developed a reputation for looking *very serious* and never closing their shop. And according to the guy with a moustache who liked to hang out near As-Salibi's apartment complex, they were always going back and forth from Israeli jail. Occasionally, they were also picked up by the Fatah-dominated Palestinian Authority, for what As-Salibi called the worst-kept secret in Bethlehem: the shop was a cover. These brothers were Hamas watchmen, reporting intelligence to their party headquarters back in Gaza.

Fidgeting a little on this fact, I backed onto the empty curb and looked across a valley at the hilltop settlement of Har Homa, the one that couldn't be seen from As-Salibi's porch. It appeared so safe behind its concrete wall, hugging the hilltop.

My mind then lurched ahead to Bil'in, and how everyone just loved to say that these Friday protests were "nonviolent." But in the West Bank, where there is a disparity between "what is" and "what is supposed to be," I knew that "nonviolent" simply meant the Palestinians wouldn't be bringing their machine guns. *What would be there instead? Jesus, man, what am I getting myself into?*

I reached down for Che, but for the first time during my entire stint in the Middle East, I was detached from my surf-board companion. *My ability to charm my way out of situations as a California surfer had been cut off. I had lost my way to explain things.*

My head was spinning as Jared came marching out of The Hamas Shop with the supplies. He flagged down a taxi and the three of us hopped in the back. As-Salibi leaned over my lap in the cab and whispered with a wicked smile, "Whenever I go into The Hamas Shop, I can't tell if those brothers want to kill me . . . or they're just rabid from getting sodomized in Israeli jail."

———

Getting to Bil'in was not an optimal travel experience. It was a headache that even the American pharmaceutical industry couldn't mend. In a place carved up by walls, green lines, blue lines, checkpoints, curfews, and everything occupation, a zig-zagging route is the only way. After the cab dropped us off in Bethlehem (just south of Jerusalem), we piled into minibuses headed to the de facto Palestinian capital of Ramallah (just north of Jerusalem).

Logically, the best way to get from Bethlehem to Ramallah was to go in a straight line through East Jerusalem, which the

Palestinians claim as the capital of their future Palestinian state. But access was denied for most Palestinians in the West Bank, since few have a Jerusalem ID card. So like most north-to-south travel in the West Bank, our minibus took a narrow, winding road that meandered almost as far inland as Jordan.

Two years ago, when I took this same winding road, I watched a truck veer too close to the edge and start a small landside. The turn had been poorly negotiated . . . though there was hardly enough road to negotiate with. Palestinian roads often give the feeling that either some careless boozer laid them out, or they were intended to yield to the nearly half million Jewish settlers who continued to build in the West Bank and East Jerusalem.

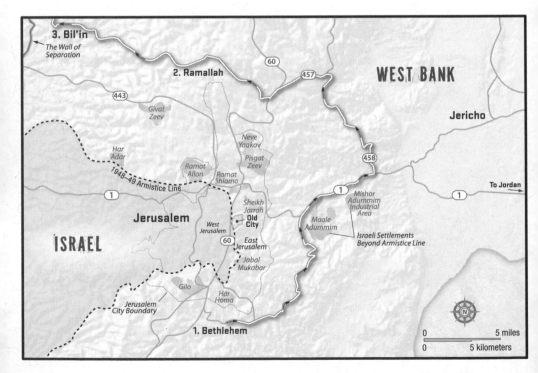

"Ri*diculous*!" said As-Salibi, hitting the "diculous" like he had just been refused a drink at some rodeo near Dallas.

Getting from Bethlehem to Ramallah should have taken 20 minutes, but it took us over an hour, and we almost hit something that looked like a goat. When we finally arrived, As-Salibi, Jared, and I desperately needed to shake off our Churning Bus Sickness . . . so we slammed another Arabic coffee, downed one of those garlic-filled *baghdi* falafels, and waited for a taxi on the road leading to Bil'in.

Jared had scored some flak jackets from the Ma'an news agency the night before. He handed one to each of us. I dropped to the curb and sat quietly with my jacket on my lap. *Are we actually going to need this?* The jacket was heavy and black. The English word "PRESS" was double-stitched on the front, stressing that it had *not* been assembled in some crude Oriental sweatshop. On the back, it said the same with the Arabic translation underneath.

I whipped the clumsy thing over my knee and beat on the chest protector. In a casual voice, I said, "So you think this could really stop a bullet?"

As-Salibi didn't hear. But Jared grinned like a true fanatic. He had been working at Ma'an for the past three years. He arrived somewhere around the time As-Salibi and I met in Nablus in 2007. And he meant business. A year or two older than As-Salibi and I, Jared had graduated from Yale. He represented the more serious strain of what I wanted to be: young, motivated, taking a hard-ass stand for things he believed in. Just one look and you could see a fine journalistic career shining ahead of him. As-Salibi once told me about when Jared pulled him aside over some small office dispute: "We work for the largest Palestinian news outlet on the West Bank. We have the *privilege* of telling these people's story to the world!" And that was Jared: full of lively passion. And perhaps the most shocking thing about Jared was that he was an American Jew who came to Israel on a Birthright trip and ended up working for a Palestinian news agency.

"Nah," said Jared, "it wouldn't stop a bullet." He dug into the front pocket, undoing the Velcro that secured the plate into the jacket. Then he held the large square up to the sun, giving it a pre-protest examination, as if his naked eye alone could detect a weakness that would let a fatal bullet through.

"Or what if they shoot us in the head?" I blurted out, hunched over and on the edge of the curb.

Jared enjoyed a savage guffaw in the day's heat. "Shoot you in the head? Ha!"

As-Salibi giggled like a loon.

Self-confidence. That—more than anything—is what keeps the war journalist returning to the front. My question was an infraction. I had posed a hypothetical worst-case scenario, just the kind of thing that might interfere with a journalist's prime directive: go into the place, get the story, and pull the fuck out before someone actually does shoot you in the head. Doubt is what actually gets people killed.

"Normally, Israeli soldiers are pretty good at shooting a warning shot in the sky." Jared was still holding the plate of the flak jacket high against the sun, checking for vulnerabilities. "But the thing to do, when they shoot the tear gas canisters, is to look up to the sky and try to see where it's going. Then . . . run like hell."

"Okay," I said, my voice cracking a little. "I understand if you guys have to get up close for the pictures, but don't take it all personally if I hang near the back for a while."

Now that I understood what could happen, I was starting to question whether or not I actually wanted to go to this protest. My stomach turned as I pictured the three of us passed out on the ground, choking on tear gas, caught in the middle of a goddamn war zone that we frankly did not need to be in.

Both Jared and I had some Jewish blood, but we weren't exactly about to grow dreadlocks and lobby for West Bank settlements. And As-Salibi? Jesus, that WASPy Texan had no connection at all to the Middle East, beyond a lust for adrenaline, coffee, and riveting storytelling. The mean old truth was that we were going to Bil'in by *choice*, knowing damn well that when the protest erupted, we couldn't ease our way through, charming both sides as American tourists. An Israeli tear gas canister or a Palestinian rock could hit us in the head no matter what "side" we were perceived to be on. Once we were in the fray, there would be no going back. No escape.

I knew the rhetoric about how some of the best decisions in life come from leaving your comfort zone for reasons you cannot name. But when I stood and picked up the flak jacket, my hand trembled.

Then the taxi showed up.

"Go where?" shouted the driver, turning his hand in the inquisitive gesture that Arab cabbies often make.

"Bil'in!" called Jared.

"Bil'in!" As-Salibi echoed.

This was my chance to abort.

Flak jackets in one hand and cameras in the other, As-Salibi and Jared eagerly piled into the back like sardines. I followed. We were going to Bil'in. Thereby agreeing to whatever was waiting down the road.

———

Jared was on the far side of the backseat, cleaning his camera lens with a careful, clockwise motion. As-Salibi was in the middle, leaning his head back and closing his eyes. I held the door handle, knowing that whatever was going to happen was going to happen faster than I could process. It was going to be explosive. Everything would feel humid and sleepy—then, striking from the other end of the adrenaline spectrum, chaos would erupt and we would have to move quickly to avoid becoming causalities of the story. *Slip in. Slip out. That was the plan.*

Driving along the winding roads on the hillsides between Ramallah and Bil'in, we passed no signs or paint to mark any kind of divide. It had that classic feeling of sleepy old Palestine. And everything seemed dehydrated. The only shade that lingered along the sun-dried hills was from olive trees: all short, stubby, and wiry, like they were wired into some kind of survival trip of their own.

Our cab hugged a few long turns and passed through several small outposts that could almost be called villages. As we pulled into Bil'in, I saw a few aged houses, an old white mosque, a non-Hamas shop, and just a few more stops to make this fine little farming town viable. The white rock, olive trees, and rolling desert hills were frankly pretty cool. To the foreign eye—that didn't know the context—Bil'in looked like just another Arab village in the Arabdom of Arab villages.

The mosque was the most significant feature of Bil'in. As soon as the muezzin finished reciting the formal Friday prayers, everything would kick into gear, and the march to The Wall and the battle of Bil'in would begin.

Jared was chatting in the street with some Palestinian guy in Arabic. He said the muezzin still had another 20 minutes left. The man then invited the three of us to his friend's house, speaking in Arabic. I picked up the word *foreigners*.

We staggered off the hot and empty street, the ever-so-modest main drag of Bil'in. Walking through someone's dirt yard, we climbed the back staircase into a second-story house. When the door slowly opened, a poster of Yasser Arafat with his queerish grin greeted us. We passed more posters of slain Fatah martyrs as we went down the hall. I wasn't sure what we were getting into. But when we came into the living room, there were ten young, 20-something Westerners, sipping tea on a circle of couches, all here on a volunteer program, not too different from what As-Salibi and I did in Nablus. Everyone was sweating in the heat.

I looked over at Jared. He seemed comfortable with the situation, but I couldn't tell if he had planned for us to meet up with these people or if he had been romping around the West Bank too long to consider this casual hookup to be out of the ordinary. Following his lead, As-Salibi and I rested our flak jackets in the far corner of the room, under another poster of Arafat, and took a seat on the couch.

In the distance, the muezzin was still deep in reciting a verse from the Holy Koran and it carried well through the second-story apartment. Slowly, we introduced ourselves, chatting here and there. The guy sitting next to me with blond hair down to his shoulders was actually a surfer from California. Even while I was talking to him, it seemed surreal, like he'd been cut out of my life back home and roughly inserted into this unlikely Palestinian scene. He didn't seem particularly strong or bold. Just a very normal dude of the surf culture. I was about to ask him what he was doing here . . . but then, the room abruptly went quiet.

Stern and commanding, a moustached Palestinian man came out from the kitchen and introduced himself. He was the leader of the organization that had brought these ten foreigners to Bil'in. He had an official village title, but between the heat and my avid anxiety about our impending entanglement with the Israeli Army, I failed to jot it down in my little black book. Everybody kept his or her eyes glued on him and he kept saying "no pictures."

Soon the stern Palestinian leader started in on the subject of tear gas. "When you are gassed, do not rub your eyes," he told us, in his thick accent. "It will only be worse."

Sitting uncomfortably cross-legged on the couch, I felt my eyebrows lift in disbelief and alarm. *When* we are gassed!?

The man paused. He pointed solemnly across the room to a bearded Palestinian-American kid from San Francisco, who stood up and addressed the group. "The stuff really isn't gas, guys. It's a fine powder. That's why rubbing makes it worse."

Pressure was building again. My body felt like it was zooming along at high speeds and then all of a sudden, stopped.

There was an eerie stillness. The muezzin had finished his call. Without a word, everyone got up and started back down the concrete stairs to the street.

In that moment it became clear that I was going to have to look after myself. All of these people had their own agendas—the stern Palestinian man; the San Francisco kid with the beard; these eager volunteers; even Jared and As-Salibi, the mighty war correspondents. But I had nothing to prove and I was there to merely absorb whatever was offered. This was not my battle to fight.

Descending slowly, I reached my left hand out, running my fingers along the cool white rock wall in the shadows of the stairwell. It felt so secure—even aged. It had rested there, impervious, for so long, refusing to take sides. It must have had quite a story to tell. I wanted to be that rock. I wanted my jittery self to sink into its calm, to take comfort and find that safe place to hide. It was perhaps one of the few things in this town that wasn't a target. Nobody looks at a rock with malicious intent . . . do they?

———

Tromping down the stairs ahead of me, Jared and As-Salibi talked business. Soon they would be dodging olive trees on the front lines, like the guerrilla journalists they were—snapping pictures and jotting down quotes to tell the world what they saw. These guys were professionals. All they ever talked about was Israel-Palestine, weighing in on the debate with every minuscule detail. For Jared and As-Salibi, it was all that mattered. Their focus was pure. Crystalline. Awake. Looking right at the conflict and never turning away . . . no surfing or smartass antics to be blended in anywhere.

I was really starting to understand the difference between them and me. The fact was, the same danger that made them

surge with adrenaline made my knees go weak. I was, quite literally, here for the ride. Ready and able to do whatever it took to
surf from Israel to Lebanon, to carve an inland route that no sane
surfer should ever care to investigate. But Jared and As-Salibi
were here for their jobs. Their salary. This was how they paid the
bills. It was their "work" to run toward the battle of Bil'in on this
Friday, no matter what the danger. And they just fuckin' loved it.

When we reached the yard, Jared saw something, glanced
at me for a second, and grinned. Reaching into the dry bushes,
he picked up a stashed sheet-metal shield. On its face was a young
Palestinian man on a neon orange background with large letters
that said, "Goodbye, Bassem. You were a friend to us."

Smiling as an expression of the craziness, As-Salibi swung
his camera off his flak-jacket-covered shoulder and took a picture as Jared held the shield in a respectful pose. "I wrote up this
story a while ago. Most people don't die in these protests, but this
guy did. Apparently some Israeli soldier shot him in the head
with a tear gas canister." *Back to shooting people in the head?*

At this point, I was starting to really feel it. Things were
happening too fast. Shit was about to go down, as advertised,
and there was nothing I could do about it. I searched inside for
meaning, but all I could find were my raw nerves, dangling by a
thread. I was scared. Barely fine. *I really didn't want to get shot and
end up on some goddamn shield!*

Jared put the shield back in the bushes and headed out to
the mosque. The streets that had been empty 20 minutes ago
were now alive with protesters beating their chests in a percus-
sive, pre-protest craze, with journalists gearing up to cover the
goddamn thing. Upon a quick glance, the two groups (protesters

and press) seemed to be represented rather equally.

Suddenly, from the loudspeakers attached to the tops of the two minarets on the mosque, the muezzin barked a guttural command—not at all like his beautiful recitation of the Koran from a few minutes before. Then a pissed-off hoard of chanting protesters roared down the road toward where I was standing. It was all inevitable now.

The Day of Protest. The march to The Wall. The battle of Bil'in. All spinning in a crazed synthesis. It was starting.

———

Living out the romantic caricature of guerrilla journalists, As-Salibi and Jared hoofed down the street with their cameras, weighed down by their flak jackets and multiple packs of cigarettes. I could hear the jackets creak wildly across their backs as they moved. It was like the sound of pack mules being whipped by some alcoholic master—but Jared and As-Salibi were the masters, covering the story, darting quickly and aggressively to be ready for what was going to happen next.

Wearing my glasses, I fully appreciated the reason the designers of the flak jacket translated "PRESS" into Arabic on the back. You could see the letters move from side to side as they ran . . . so a potential gunner, who'd have the best shot at them from this angle, would know that they were noncombatants. I turned then, scouring the mob for weapons, but saw none. No arms here. Not even a lone nut in the back with a Kalashnikov. And none of these people would shoot them anyway, as Jared and As-Salibi were clearly reporting for the Palestinian side.

Wailing over a bullhorn, some protesting soul shouted, *"Filistin Arabya!"* It was a famous chant I had heard a thousand times before. It's reported that Saddam Hussein uttered *"Filistin Arabya"* ("Palestine is Arab") as his last words before the Mahdi Army noosed his neck in Iraq. Even if Saddam did utter the phrase, he wasn't the first. Though saying it made people question the possibility that Saddam was the only Arab leader with the power to reunite the Arabs. Of course, the Palestinians wouldn't have liked answering to Saddam, but there must have been some comfort in the idea that an Arab leader had reserved his final words for their cause. Even in the Arab world, the Palestinians aren't used to a whole lot of support. They are used to being treated like, well . . . *Palestinians.*

With *"Filistin Arabya"* ringing in the air, I ducked my head and ran to catch up with the boys. They were actually a few hundred yards *in front of* the protest. Just as I joined the crowd, a Chevy with **"PRESS REUTERS"** painted in red letters on the hood burst out of a side street at high speed, missing the mob by a hair.

Crouching down abruptly behind a white brick wall, covered with green and red Arabic graffiti, I lay low and snapped pictures. The crowd's size had doubled, and they were marching onward to The Wall.

Someone in the main horde had brought a drum, another a bullhorn. People were yelling a myriad of things in a myriad of languages. I crouched down even lower, but not so low as to hide the "PRESS" stitching on my flak jacket. The situation felt so combustible that I thought the most important thing was to keep my jacket high, so everyone could see my business for being there: PRESS!!!!!!

In the distance, out in the open, Jared and As-Salibi were standing under one of the larger olive trees, adjacent to where the PRESS REUTERS Chevy was now parked.

Quivering like a fiend, I kept adjusting my elevation near the wall, trying to figure out exactly how low—or how high—I should squat as the Bil'in mob approached. *Would the gas just come out of nowhere? How would this work?*

Once I ducked down too fast and the left knee of my worn blue jeans tore. *Fuck! Instead of taking photos, I'll switch my camera to video and shoot the mob passing.*

And slowly, they did: old Palestinian men in bland suits and white checkered keffiyehs, middle-aged men with Palestinian flags attached to broomsticks (one carrying the shield of his fallen comrade), kids whose mothers had wrapped their faces with scarves for the gas. And then there were the Westerners. The surfer with long blond hair that I'd met in the stern Palestinian man's apartment strolled by, wearing his surf sandals, shorts, and some kind of ridiculous name-brand sunglasses. He looked like he was headed to some drunken beach bash in San Diego.

Right next to me, an older Palestinian-American man, dressed like an Asian tourist, popped up out of nowhere. He started to speak, fidgeting with his geeky camera utility belt. "This is the valley. If you don't want to get teargassed, don't go in there. There is some wind today and it blows down the wadi. The Israelis can cover the whole valley with gas, *if they want to.*"

I knew what he meant. The Wall—no more than double barbed-wire fence here—was positioned just over the top of the other side of the wadi. Whenever the mob approached, the Israeli military could easily shoot over their heads and sandwich them in between The Wall and the dip in the small river valley they had crossed. On the top of the wadi, there was another road that ran a few hundred yards adjacent to the protesters' route through the dip in the wadi, making them vulnerable to a clandestine side operation by Israeli commandos.

I took it all in from the top of the valley, lined with olive trees and that classic Levantine white rock. It was clear that the Israelis not only had all the military equipment and training, but the high ground—which they constructed with their Wall and roads—to trap the protesters and eventually gas them to smithereens. It was mad to enter this valley. But then again, the Palestinians must have figured, who the fuck cares? This whole twisted thing was based on a mad premise!

The protesters continued yelling nationalist slogans and beating their chests, as the small army of journalists snapped pictures and prepared themselves for the ironic Israeli cure: gas.

I could see Jared and As-Salibi marching quickly down the long, roughly paved road that crossed the wadi to The Wall. As the crowd continued to approach, I kept snapping pictures of them gearing up for the danger they were venturing into. I had some distance from the cresting boom of energy that pushed the mob forward; still, I felt its intensity dead-on. An emotional tide was fueling this wave, a rage that churned against the people who had stolen their farmland, their villages, and their economy.

At the very bottom of the wadi, before it started up to The Wall, I picked a position on a rock. The mob had taken formation now. Their unity in the moment had turned a horde of grab-ass Arabs into an impassioned band of protestors with one sole purpose: show the world the inhumanity and injustice of the West Bank.

The man leading the charge sat in a wheelchair. His legs were atrophied. And looking at him, it was easy to tell that this was no General Vespasian on a Roman chariot, but more like a Maxwell Shrimperton character. With one hand on the brake and the other on the surgeon's mask he wore, he slowly wove along the poorly paved road, marred with black grenade stains and mounds of exploded tear gas canisters from some previous time.

He had no weapons, no means of inflicting any sort of physical damage on the Israeli soldiers. The idea was to look as Gandhi as possible. And that was his strength. For his weapons were the journalists. Without a doubt, they would capture this essence of human decency, which would trigger revulsion in viewers when the picture appeared all over the Internet in a few hours. This man would make the Israelis, with their American-funded vehicles and equipment, look like a band of ruthless war criminals by comparison. That was the point.

No doubt the Israeli-Palestinian conflict is waged by raids, walls, and suicide bombers. But The Day of Protest was about broadcasting to the world. The people of Bil'in got that and knew the best thing they could do to get their land back was to cause as much of a scene as humanly possible.

From the rock I was on, I saw the crowd pause long enough for the small army of journalists, fortified behind rocks and olive trees, to snap cover-story shots of this small, lonely Palestinian cripple, wheeling himself out, like David to meet Goliath. Only this time, Goliath was a Jew.

By the time I got to The Wall, some of the men from the Palestinian villages had lit a tire on fire, which emitted black smoke for the cameras. Others were tearing at the barbed wire, in a largely symbolic gesture. Most of the young boys were high on the adjacent slope, hurling rocks at a few fully-armed Israeli soldiers, who surely looked on camera like the shameless enforcers at the Kent State massacre in 1970. The journalists were taking pictures. The foreigners were making comments to each other, trying desperately to understand how twisted this world could be. The few Palestinian women who showed up were breaking from their Islamic reserve by yelling at their men to not wimp out while they looked for a subtle trouble of their own.

It was unlike any moment I had ever seen. In a way it was more intense than Nablus in 2007, because of the looming inevitability of Israeli retaliation. I could literally see them load their tear gas guns on the other side.

But there were no arms on this side of The Wall. Only Palestinian kids throwing rocks, older dudes lighting another tire on fire, and others tearing at The Wall in a way that was majorly provocative. I understood what the Israelis did to Bil'in's viability, but in simple terms, no military occupation in the world could tolerate this kind of aggression. It couldn't let this sort of nonviolence stand.

Jared and As-Salibi would later remind me (again and again) that the Israelis had illegally crossed the Green Line and annexed half the village. Thus, it was perfectly understandable that the people would hurl a few rocks. "Things here," said Jared and As-Salibi, "were way past nonviolence . . ."

The real surprise to me that day was not the clashing of Israelis and Palestinians. It was the Ashkenazi Israeli man standing in protest with the Palestinians. I saw a Palestinian man, who had been yelling "1, 2, 3, 4, Occupation No More!" over his bullhorn, walk over to the old Jew and offer him the opportunity to heckle.

Accepting the horn, the old man introduced himself to the armed Israeli soldiers across the sea of barbed wire. He said he fought for Israel in the Sinai during the Six-Day War. But he was against this occupation by his own countrymen.

"You are taking their land!" he shouted to the young soldiers with vehemence. "Look at them! They are peacefully protesting and you are about to gas them?!"

When I was in Haifa and on my Birthright Israel trip before that, I had met Israelis who were opposed to the occupation, but it seemed like treason to go against the army. The Israeli man was speaking in English, so the Palestinians, the young Israelis in uniform, and the horde of foreigner onlookers could understand. "I am from Tel Aviv. I am Israeli! Why are you doing this? Look at them!"

As he went on, trying to reason with them, I noticed the hysteria of the protest was on the rise. Through the soldiers' Plexiglas shields I could see that they were visibly shaken. Not good.

If the Palestinian men actually made any progress in ripping down the barbed-wire fence, the soldiers would jump out from behind their trucks and rush through small corridors in the barbed wire, forcing the Palestinian men to flee the wrath of their batons. If things got out of hand, the Israelis would have to respond with real military force. They had to show that it was unacceptable to tear down Their Wall for Their Occupation. Plain and simple, the Israeli Army had to enforce things. If they weren't willing to do that, then the whole conflict would be over.

But the unruly mob of Bil'in knew exactly what it was doing. In the twenty-first century, even oppressed villagers in an occupied territory understand the importance of a "photo op." The protestors were acutely attuned to the fact that this little Friday skirmish was only hours away from making international news. And that was the handle: if the Israeli Army were ever to move The Wall, it wouldn't be the result of rioting villagers but of a coalition of Western states that decided to make a big deal out of it. Which led me to think, *even if they somehow got their land back, would they still be farmers?* This was a calculated PR campaign and they were proving to be the masters.

Then, the gas came: *Phewboom! Phewboom!*

It was like a frenzied herd of pachyderms came storming down the wadi. It was the kind of savage chaos only triggered in humans when they are put in a situation of life and death; when the animal brain takes over, and intellect is just a cumbersome waste of time. For the Bil'in mob, there was no sort of method in this moment. No sort of formation. Just a stampede of wild brutes, all fleeing and running manically, and for the lone safety of the individual. A true state of nature.

Off the bat I knew that this *phewboom* sound was not a gunshot. As-Salibi's porch in Nablus had taught me that. This sound was too hollow. And indeed, it came from a set of dueling American CS tear gas canisters, launched upwind to beat back the protesting mob so the Israeli soldiers could safely approach and secure their torn-at fence.

I was at the back of the mob, near the bottom of the wadi, when I saw As-Salibi come crashing down in a tearing state of hysteria.

And like an inquisitive prick, I flicked my camera to video and took aim: "What happened, Salibi?"

His eyes were bloodshot and his shirt soaked in sweat. His face was Valentine's Day red, but there was no romance here. It held revulsion.

"Shit got out of hand, man . . . shit always gets out of hand around here."

He was panting hard. He turned away in a state of gassed misery, not really comprehending that he was being filmed. He then looked up at the chaos behind him and stumbled back to take more pictures. Journalistic autopilot had taken over. He was going back to the front.

I walked down the road that led back into the river valley. Higher in the wadi, I could see some Palestinian teenagers throwing rocks at what looked to be a second front of the protest. As I drew closer, I could see that they were throwing them at two Israelis soldiers, standing in full body armor next to their trucks, on the other side of the chain-link fence. The Palestinian teens were very close to the soldiers, and I could hear the Israelis trying to reason with them, lecturing them condescendingly, as an American cop might do with juvenile delinquents. But this wasn't about smoking grass on school grounds; this was about land and who got to live on it.

Eager to hear what these Israeli soldiers were saying, I ran off the paved road and ventured up the wadi to investigate, hoofing it up and over rocks, squeezing between olive trees, but staying low—hidden as much as possible.

Though I had a hard time hearing, and my Arabic wasn't nearly good enough, I could get a healthy dose of what was being said by body language:

Armored Israeli soldier:

> Look, kid, I'm armed by the United States and I have all that kind of fury standing behind me: trucks, armor, nonlethal and lethal weapons, M16s, Merkava tanks, gunships, and a mean motherfucker of a nuclear site at Dimona. There just isn't a chance you're going to win today . . . so why don't you do us all a favor and go back to your little village?

Palestinian kids:

> Gladly. As soon as you stop taking our land, you fools! Don't you see? After Operation Cast Lead, when you killed almost 2,000 Gazans in a month, the world thinks differently of you now! The Goldstone Report! The South African Jew who said that "both sides" might have committed war crimes . . . meaning you, too! And by using anything in your arsenal, you are falling victim to your own problem: you got kicked out of Europe and now kick us out of our farmland in Palestine!

My muscles were tight, and I continued to feel the fear of being discovered. It was a long way back across the exposed field to the main road, and if things started to escalate, it would take a good minute to get back. I was starting to feel isolated, like it might have been a really bad fucking idea to have left the mob. My foot slid a little, forcing my right shoe off the rock it was resting on and letting me know that my balance wasn't what it had been.

"Hey, you!" yelled one of the Israeli soldiers in English. I had been spotted. The armed soldier stopped heckling the Palestinian kids and pointed his black-gloved finger definitely in my direction.

There was no time to explain things, so . . . I ran like hell. An olive branch hit my cheek and broke the skin as I jumped from rock to rock, nearly slipping. Dry brush seemed to always be in the way. As I nearly tumbled onto the broken pavement of the road, panting in a sort of manic dehydration, I felt sweat dripping off of me. Everything was hot and dizzy.

My only hope was to keep moving back to the front, working my way into the crowd and blending into the anonymity of protesters. I pushed my way into a horde of local people and stood there, with dry lips. And then, I laughed, letting out a deep breath of absurdity.

What if those guys knew me? What if underneath all that armor, that one who yelled at me was one of those soldiers I'd met on the Birthright trip? Maybe he recognized me and wanted to know how the surf was in Haifa. It was only a few weeks ago that I was sitting next to these guys on a bus, touring around, partying, and chasing girls together.

Just as I caught my breath, a hundred *phewbooms* bombarded the upper wadi, taking no aim, holding all prisoner. It was the gassing to end the gassing. Simple. Crisp. Predictable. Toxic to the concept of life. The Birthright memories and relief were over.

All around me people were running and crying, their faces twisted in agony as if the fires of hell had rained down upon them. Everyone was an individual again, wailing to the same gassing but in a completely different way. Some were sniffing rags with alcohol; others were washing their faces with water, cursing and taking shade beneath the same olive tree that once had the **PRESS REUTERS** Chevy parked under it.

The protest was over. Everyone was recovering, making the stumble home. No different than at this time on any previous Friday . . . and probably the next one.

———————

Back at the apartment, I dropped my stuff on the floor. I had made my way back to Bethlehem with Jared and As-Salibi, and we parted in front of The Hamas Shop. They were headed into the office to write up the story. I couldn't think of doing such a thing. There was nothing left in my energy reserves and my adrenaline glands were dry. Unlike Jared and As-Salibi, this was the first time my skin had been covered with the fine white powder of the gas, and I needed to get it off. On the way to As-Salibi's bathroom, I caught my reflection in the mirror. I looked like I'd been swept up in a sandstorm and tossed from its fiery anus.

Stunned and overwhelmed, I walked into the shower with all my clothes on. Holding the walls, I let the cold water numb my irritated flesh. At first, there was nothing in my head. But then, the scene started to reappear from after the gassing—*in third person, and real time*—when everyone was walking back to Bil'in.

From the corner of his eye, the Journalist-Surfer sees the Israeli man from the Six-Day War, just after a spiraling tear gas canister falls from the sky and ravages his face with a direct spray.

The man's tear ducts are in overdrive, desperately trying to flush his own country's mace from his eyes. He drops to a knee on the broken West Bank pavement, and quivers in deep and agonizing pain. For a moment, he aimlessly swings his arms through the open air, searching for a balance he cannot find—he cannot see. His face is chapped and red. He is trying to get up, but he can only stay down.

Out of the corner of his other eye, the Journalist-Surfer sees the same Palestinian from the pre-protest apartment walk over to the crouched Israeli.

Is this a problem? the Journalist-Surfer wonders.

"Shalom aleichem," says the hard Palestinian man in Hebrew. "May peace be upon you." He then reaches for the Israeli's hand, gently lifting his pained brother, and the Arab and the Jew walk back to the small West Bank village of Bil'in. Together.

And so was the gassing at Bil'in.

TWENTY-FIVE-STEP PROGRAM: BETHLEHEM TO BEIRUT

Black cat cross my path
I think every day is going to be my last.

NINA SIMONE, "Mississippi Goddamn"

The day after my West Bank gassing I took a Sabbath. I probably was the only goon in Palestinian Bethlehem to observe the Jewish day of rest, but what the hell? I needed the time and the space. The gassing had left me downright exhausted—to the point that I didn't even realize the pirated DVD I was watching was in Russian . . . until after the goddamn alien invasion of South Africa. The West Bank's a hell of a place to watch *District 9*.

But no effort could be spent on cinema. This was about recovery. And I needed all the recovery I could get before the next leg of my journey: from Bethlehem to Beirut. This would be the true test of whether surfing from Israel to Lebanon was even achievable. After all.

From Haifa to Beirut is 78 miles. From Bethlehem, Beirut is about 150 miles. And to the conventional numbers nerd, I was now farther from my Beiruti destination. But that's what makes the Middle East so damn interesting—the numbers nerd is wrong. All distance is calculated on the whim of old grudges and strange politics: *what papers require how much waiting at what border.* This is key.

After the First World War, when Western colonial powers helped divide the Middle East into nation-states, people traveled on the ability of The Common Ass. In 1868, Mark Twain claimed that Palestine could be crossed—on The Common Ass—in under a week. But eventually, when cars, airplanes, and paved roads were introduced, The Asses were freed, and all Levantine capitals could be reached within a day. And in 1973, U.S. Secretary of State Henry Kissinger did just that.

With the permission of both Israel and the Arab states, Kissinger moved freely, holding swift meetings that ended the fourth Arab-Israeli war. This became known as shuttle diplomacy. And while Kissinger's ability to quickly hold talks in various capitals proved to be a success, another thing happened that mustn't be forgotten: people remembered that what used to take The Common Ass a week was now possible in an hour's flight or afternoon's cruise. The only problem was you had to be Henry Kissinger to do it.

So perhaps that's why people study the Middle East: with all the closed borders and wars and checkpoints of today, my route—from Israel to Lebanon—might have been faster with Mark Twain and his horde of asses, over 140 years ago.

———

But back to the matter at hand: there is honestly no way to describe the dreadful dizziness and endless zigzags that it took

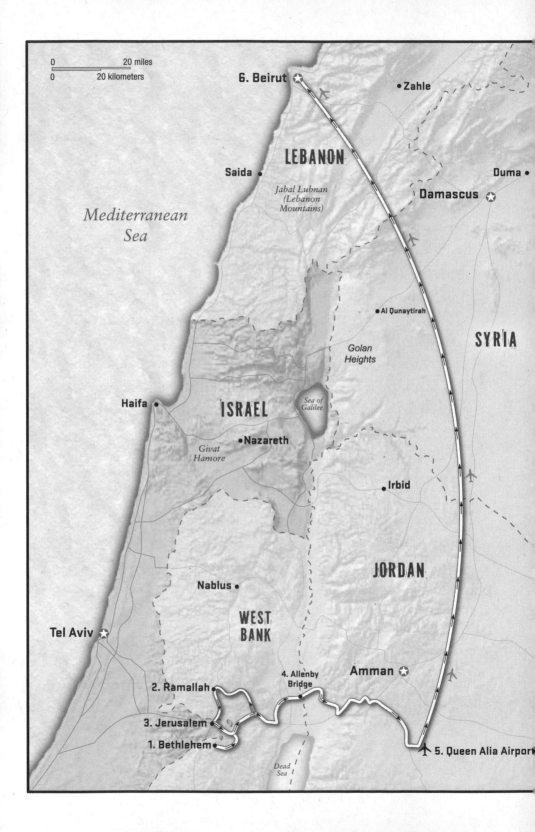

to travel from Bethlehem to Beirut in one grueling day. There weren't just crazy things happening, but a collection of crazy things, often collaborating with each other in a sort of crazy things synthesis . . . giving a new definition to chaos. It's like what Stalin said about the Soviet economy: "2 + 2 = 5." And like the Soviet economy, nothing was ever on the same page.

To get from Bethlehem to Beirut I would have to carry four separate identities; four separate stories; four sets of visas, both entry and exit; four sets of currency; three different bus schedules; two passports, with an ability to conceal one of them; a flight schedule; and the fuckin' charm to come off as a sincere connoisseur of Middle Eastern surfing.

To do this mind job any sort of justice, I had to dive straight into my sickly, chicken-scratched notes and translate them verbatim. The following is a mixture of notes and words put to pictures amassed on my journey from Bethlehem to Beirut. It is madly twisted but the closest thing to a literal account of what happened—in case there's anyone out there who wishes to attempt this surfing stunt. Make no mistake: this section is best read high on caffeine with "Love Me Two Times," by The Doors abusing your eardrums.

1.   Sunday. Alarm jingles at 6:00 a.m. Make Arabic coffee on As-Salibi's brown stove. Watch it spill over with indifference. Eat two-day-old bread. Also with indifference. Shake the lousy journalist in his bed good-bye. Thank him for teargassing and slap twisted fucker on the cheek. Slam iron door at 6:45 a.m. Call

cabbie. Greet cabbie. Lower front seat. Slide Che in. The Surfboard Trick!

2. Arrive at Bethlehem bus station at 7:30 a.m. Slam coffee from vendor. Pay the scheming bastard. Tell vendor, "Going to Beirut." Vendor says, "Impossible!" Grin madly. Walk up to eight-seater van going to Ramallah. Get in. Pass through two Israeli checkpoints. Nobody asks about Che. Bam! No hassles.

3. Get to Ramallah at 9:30 a.m. Take taxi to Jordanian consulate for visa. "No Jordan visa," he says. "Pay only in Jordanian pounds." Walk across street to bank. Walk back. Pay in pounds. Get visa. 11:00 a.m.

4. Meet German-Palestinian dude outside consulate. Says bus to Allenby Bridge (crossing from Israel to Jordan) will take four hours from Ramallah because it takes "Palestinian roads." Insists Che and I follow him on local bus to downtown Ramallah.

5. Bus leaves Ramallah at noon. Che and I pile into far backseat. Get to Qalandia checkpoint at 12:12 p.m. Ramallah side of Jerusalem. Get off bus. Follow everyone into checkpoint. Wave American passport to Israeli guard. *Beeeeep!* Guard boots Che and me through gate. Walk ten paces. Put Che and bag on

X-ray machine. Pick up KLUTZY BASTARD on other side. Go to exit. No bus. 1:00 p.m. Next bus arrives at 1:05 p.m. Confusion.

6. Get to unknown Jerusalem bus station. 1:23 p.m. Che's strapped on one shoulder. Bag's on other. Ask five people about bus to Allenby Bridge. No one speaks English/knows/cares. 1:34 p.m. Lebanon cannot seem farther away.

7. Walk downhill with Che and bag. Arrive at Damascus Gate at 1:48 p.m. Walk by same row of cabbies As-Salibi negotiated with. "Missed last bus," says cabbie with grin. Price: 130 shekels. Leave Damascus Gate at 2:03 p.m. Cabbie/California surfer take fast Israeli roads to Jordanian border.

8. Pre-border Israeli checkpoint. 2:43 p.m. "What is that?" asks Israeli guard. "A surfboard," I say. Israeli shrugs with confusion. Taps on Che through cushioned board bag. Talks it over with other guard, lights up cigarette. Waves cabbie/California surfer/Che through. 3:00 p.m.

9. Cabbie gets to random building in desert near Jordan. "Here," he says. The edge of Israel. 3:07 p.m. Three Israeli guards approach. Take Che out of bag for

inspection. They ask, "Why surfboard in the desert?" They shrug indifferently. Confusion. 3:15 p.m.

10. Enter Israeli border checkpoint. "Just flying out of Jordan," I say. Pay 150 shekels in Israeli exit fee. Che and bag disappear for "inspection." Wait outside with other travelers going to Jordan. 3:30 p.m. 108 degrees Fahrenheit. No explanation for anything. Just "bus is coming." *But to where?* Never been to Jordan before.

11. Spend last Israeli shekels on ice cream at 3:35 p.m. Walk outside. 3:36 p.m. Ice cream melts.

12. Sit on regular bench. Listen to other travelers complain about heat. 4:35 p.m., bus shows up. Slide Che and bag underneath. No fee to get on. Curious. Start talking to strangers again. Two men are American "arms contractors." Seem to be Southern bucolic hillbillies. *Nascar!* "Helping Jordanians defend themselves." Very Donald Rumsfeld.

13. Bus drives over Allenby Bridge at 4:38 p.m. Leaves Israel. Enters Jordan. Allenby is only Israeli-Jordanian border crossing that requires visa for Americans.

14. Moustached Jordanian agents board bus. Visas inspected. Money paid. Exact change only. Defense

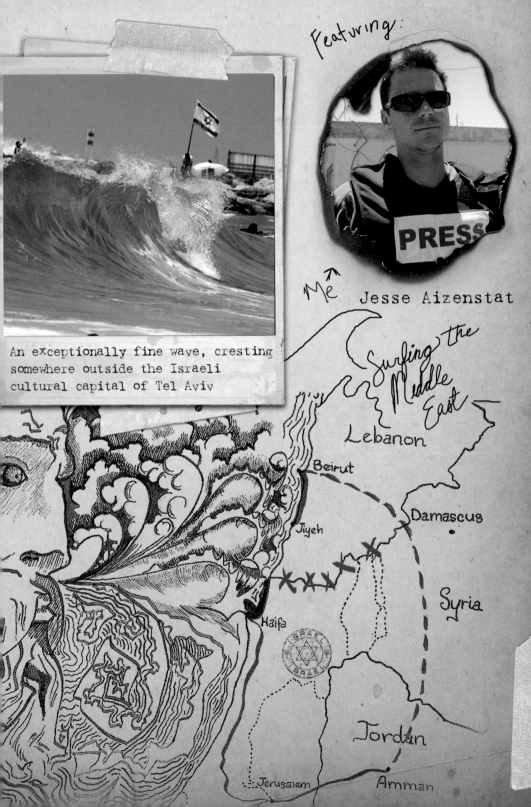

Featuring:

PRESS

Me

Jesse Aizenstat

An exceptionally fine wave, cresting
somewhere outside the Israeli
cultural capital of Tel Aviv

Surfing the Middle East

Lebanon

Beirut

Damascus

Jiyeh

Syria

Haifa

ISRAEL

Jordan

Jerusalem

Amman

First Leg

Damascus

Jiyeh

Haifa

This is Lee

Aviv Vaknin-by Yanai(Haifa_Israel)

Moving through Israel

Haifa grommet on a small day

The historic anchor
we just pulled up
from the sea

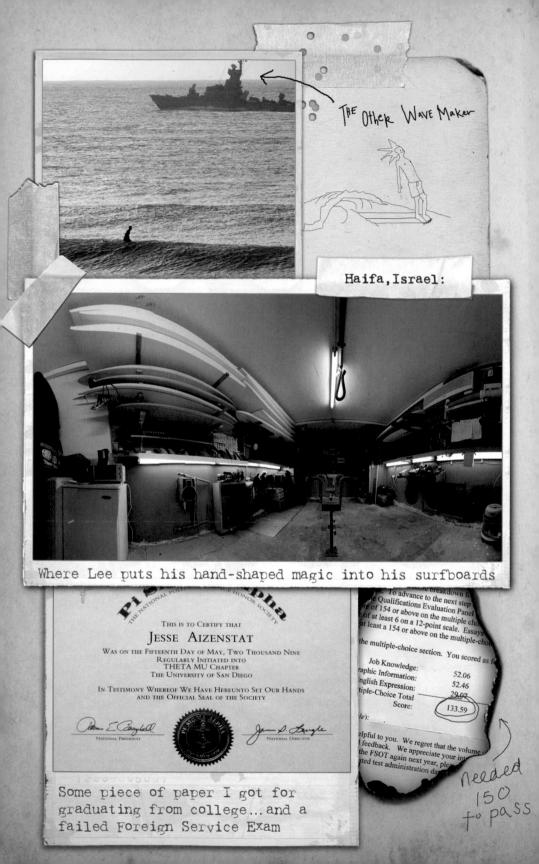

The Other Wave Maker

Haifa, Israel:

Where Lee puts his hand-shaped magic into his surfboards

Some piece of paper I got for
graduating from college...and a
failed Foreign Service Exam

. To advance to the next step
he Qualifications Evaluation Panel
e of 154 or above on the multiple cho
e of at least 6 on a 12-point scale. Essays
at least a 154 or above on the multiple-choi

the multiple-choice section. You scored as fo

Job Knowledge:
raphic Information: 52.06
nglish Expression: 52.46
ltiple-Choice Total   29.07
          Score: 133.59

le):

lpful to you. We regret that the volume o
l feedback. We appreciate your int
the FSOT again next year, ple
ated test administration da

needed
150
to pass

I put a stomp pad of "Che" on the back of my surfboard for one simple reason: keep the humor. Nothing could have kept me more safe than preserving the lighthearted spirit of the surfer.

me

"The Surfboard Trick": Convincing some Israeli cabbie that the surfboard goes in better with the front seat down is no easy thing. But it's the only way to travel. Just look in the rearview mirror.

Carmel Beach Lifeguard Tower

Baha'i Gardens, Haifa, Israel

A few days before the
Hamas/Fatah infighting,
As-Salibi and Gingy in
our apartment, Nablus,
2007

A wave-covering "shack" that, if
entered, will never be forgotten

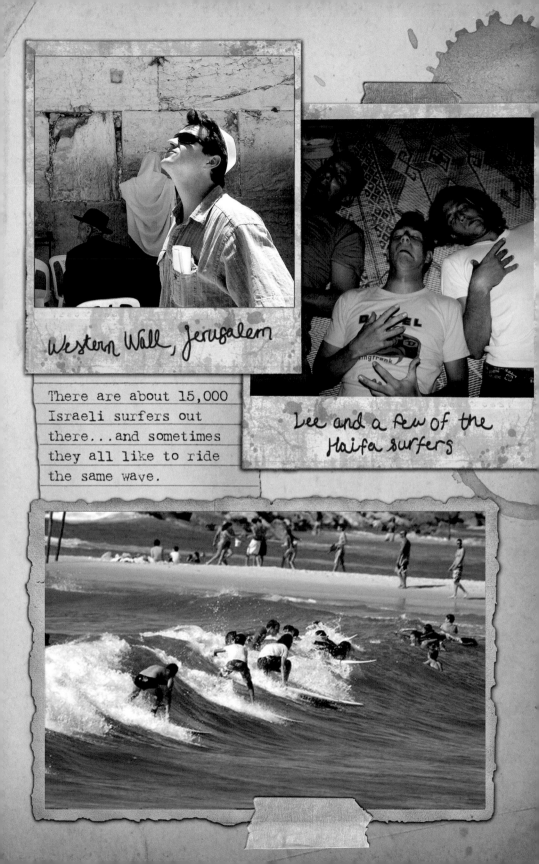

Western Wall, Jerusalem

There are about 15,000
Israeli surfers out
there...and sometimes
they all like to ride
the same wave.

Lee and a few of the
Haifa surfers

East Jerusalem cabbies arguing about the best way to tie a surfboard to the roof

Haifa

Jor

Second Leg

Jerusalem

A

Walking Che through Jaffa Street

Jerusalem and West Bank checkpoints

"Goodbye, Bassem." This was the protester who was killed by a tear gas canister.

The man leading the protest to the Wall in the West Bank village of Bil'in

Taken from As-Salibi's Bethlehem porch. West Bank apartment buildings look huddled in for protection, don't they?

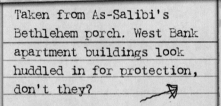

Gas Mask!!!

marching to the WALL

The Wall that divides the village of Bil'in

AS-SALIBI AND JARED GEARING UP FOR THE Battle OF Bil'in ↑

Har Homa, the Israeli settlement you can see from Bethlehem

As-Salibi sweatin'

GASSED!!!

Watching from under a West Bank olive tree

Third Leg

Lebanon

Beirut

Jiyeh

Da...

Haifa

Hitchhiking through South Lebanon

The Lebanese Lebowski

Manner drifting toward the Jiyeh Sandbars

Hezbollah mock street rockets pointed south

This is Me

Ready to score some waves with a sea-crusted civil war ship

Jiyeh wave with the refinery, blown in the 2006 war. With oil everywhere, the place had been closed for surfing.

Jammin' down the line

Hezbollah Youth

On August 14, 2009,
Hezbollah held a
rally to "remember
the martyrs" of the
2006 war. & a few
friends and I
snuck in!

HASSAN NASRALLAH,
Secretary General
of Hezbollah

The Lebanese keep their blown
buildings around to remind
everyone of the civil war.

Sharing a cab with
hot Palestinian girls
is never a bad thing.

The day Columb, the
Meccan, and I went to
track down a Jewish
synagogue in downtown
Beirut

we Found
it

Magen Avraham synagogue was badly damaged during Lebanese civil war.

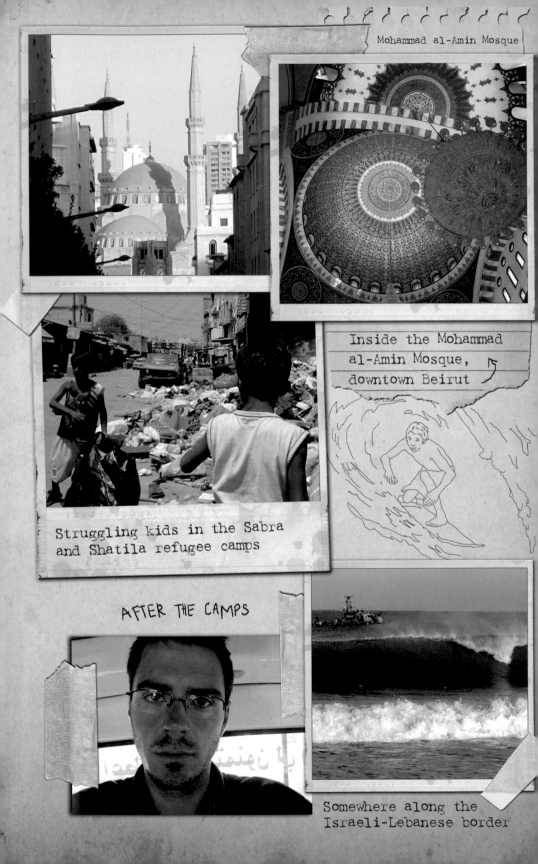

Mohammad al-Amin Mosque

Inside the Mohammad al-Amin Mosque, downtown Beirut

Struggling kids in the Sabra and Shatila refugee camps

AFTER THE CAMPS

Somewhere along the Israeli-Lebanese border

contractors help make change . . . then offer ride to airport in nice new van.

15. Contractors offer me job. Take their card. Explain surf stunt from Israel to Lebanon. Enjoy boisterous laugher. No more job talk. Vulgar language; hooker stories. Get to Queen Alia Airport in Jordan. Thank 'em *hugely*. Utter "No prob" in Southern drawl. Van speeds to next terminal. Never see them again.

16. Arrive at airport at 5 p.m. for my 8 p.m. flight. Check Che in. Nervous: A) because the Jordanians didn't charge me for Che, and B) because they didn't ask a single question about it. Make check-in guy slap *two* "handle with care" stickers on Che . . . though no Arabic translation on sticker.

17. Walk around Queen Alia airport w/out Che. Mixture of near-naked women in shop posters and fully veiled women looking at 'em. Strangeness. Flights to Saudi. Everyone clearly going to Very Islamic Place. No room for Aizenstat Smartassery.

18. Walk around more. Read. Write email to sister, also named Alia. The Jordanians read the Dune novels? At 7:50 p.m., get on plane. At 8:34 p.m., wheels lift from Hashemite Kingdom of Jordan . . . only in

Jordan 2 hours and 57 minutes. Plane bound for Republic of Lebanon. Fly *over* wait-all-day-at-border-if-you-are-American Syria.

19. Carefully switch in flight to "other" American passport—one without initial Israeli visa, Israeli Allenby exit stamp, and Jordanian entry visa/stamp. All this proof of being in *Israel*. Immediate denial of entry into Lebanon. Slide stamped passport in back pocket. Remember As-Salibi's talk on Bethlehem porch: "They Never Check The Back Pocket!" Safest place.

20. Land in Beirut. No idea of time; don't care anymore. Walk up to Lebanese immigration desk. Lebanese guard waves me forward. "No sir, I have never been to Israel . . . just flew into Jordan from . . ." But I fucked up! Needed Jordanians to stamp visa at airport to prove *how* I got to Middle East.

21. "Sweet Jesus," I think. But guard doesn't question blank second passport, valid only for two years. Guard stamps it. Gives "one-month tourist visa." Yes!

22. Walk out of terminal. Nicely dressed Lebanese man waiting for me with sign with Jewish-sounding name written in clear, bold letters: "Jesse Aizenstat." I had

forgotten . . . Lebanese American University sent guy to pick me up. Nerves nearly shot.

23. *Exhaustion.* Lower seat in his car. The Surfboard Trick! Drive through tunnel to Beirut. Get abrupt feeling: last time I was here it was in early 2007 and a tank was positioned right at the opening of this tunnel! Get to apartment.

24. Opening Che from bag. Suspect he might be dinged—from Bethlehem cab, walk to bus station after Jordanian consulate, gate at Israeli checkpoint, Jerusalem-to-Allenby cab front seat, Allenby bus, contractors' van, Royal Jordanian baggage packers, Lebanese airport, Beiruti cab. But old Che is just how I remembered: smooth, dingless, beautiful.

25. Sit on bed. Take deep breath. Look at Che, bag, self in mirror. "Wow," I say. "Here. *We are here.*"

تقدمة أهالي الجبة

Pausing for a moment while making my way through Hezbollah-controlled South Lebanon

THIRD LEG

UNSIMPLY, LEBANON

Democracy don't rule the world
You'd better get that in your head
This world is ruled by violence
But I guess that's better left unsaid

BOB DYLAN, "Union Sundown"

SURFING THE CASBAH, AUGUST 2, 2009

It's hard to get in tune when they're booing.

BOB DYLAN, 1965 tour

As events unfolded on this journey, I published notes and pictures on my blog. Most of this material reflected the crazed, in-the-moment experience that can get too refined in the reflective analysis that goes into book writing. So in the interest of keeping it real, I wrote the following blog post in my apartment in West Beirut, just before my first morning of Lebanese surfing.

It had been two teeth-grinding weeks since I landed in the Lebanese capital, still with no surf to speak of. But with the offshore buoys starting to shake, my adrenaline was pumping; I knew my first shot at Lebanese surfing was near. In order to preserve its peculiar spirit, this blog post has been left mostly in its original form. It's the jangled rant of any foreign journalist in Beirut, the tangled reasoning of someone who has found himself in a very strange place.

August 2, 2009, blog — Dawn is approaching in Beirut now; it's 5:00 a.m. Not that I looked at my watch or anything—I don't own one—but the menacing fucking chorus of those goddamn cabbies, laying on their decadent fucking horns, is a sort of ritual at this hour: dawn is coming, motherfuckers . . . Lock & Load!

But those mornings have passed from Beirut . . . or so says every faction of this impossibly feudal country—left like the blown-out buildings that still surround my apartment here in West Beirut. The Lebanese say they keep them around—the blown buildings—as a token of history, to cast a shadow, remembering (but mostly reminding everyone of) the brutish reality of what it would mean to fall back into the loathing chaos of the civil war.

"Nobody wants that," says my Shia Arabic teacher. He is from the south of the country, from a neighborhood filled with posters of slain Hezbollah martyrs. And he says he hates living there. Populous swine from "The Party of God" harass him constantly for working in mostly Sunni West Beirut, bringing home the bacon by teaching a clueless band of dumbass Americans Arabic at the Lebanese American University. But he doesn't seem too worried about it this summer. "Even if we go back to civil war this summer," my scoundrel teacher jokes, "I remember the bars that stay open . . . like the last time, I know where to hide."

Yeah . . . my Arabic teacher is one charm-hell of a scoundrel, all right. He's the kind of chap who would be your standard goof of a professor in the States, but because he's from Lebanon—the most savagely run, tribal, cutthroat, Mafia place I've ever been—he's blessed with a sort of dark humor that makes you ponder the intellectual meaning of it all. And at the Duke of Wellington (a classic British-themed pub in West Beirut), you can find him pondering. You'll know when you see him—sitting on a barstool, full of boisterous jokes, with stunningly pronounced sappiness and a queer grin that makes old Arafat look like a stiff. It's his cathartic way of being that's just so damn Lebanese. So if you're reading this in West Beirut within 30 years from when I'm hammering it out Right Now, head on down to the Duke! Order the big beer (*kabira* in Arabic). "Since the civil war," my Arabic teacher jokes, "I don't bother with the small ones."

———

But it's more than just guns & beer in Beirut these days. I've been stuck, pondering my own mean sense of bummer: THERE'S NO SURF. It's flat as a goddamn pancake. So it must have been straight luck when I hooked up with Lee and the Haifa surfers in northern Israel. I just showed up and we started surfing. How could it have been easier?

Though a similar sort of "Port Inn situation" did happen when I landed here in Beirut a few weeks ago: the "floor monitor" of my tenth-floor dorm/apartment thing saw my surfboard and also had "a friend who surfs." But I had a hard time believing him . . . as this Lebanese-American "floor monitor" was the type of flamboyant homosexual who exercised that touchy-feely thing so deliberately that nobody in the building could fathom anything but appeasement. And the best part? Nobody around here even thinks he's gay . . . No Sir! Gayness is too sphinctered in Arab culture to even be considered an option. If even rumored, his family could be greatly smeared and some crazy blood feud might come out of it or something.

The only way to prove an Arab is gay is for someone to catch the person at one of those sodomy orgies Victorian Brits liked to write about. But anyway, knowing the floor monitor was gay didn't take a college degree. The genius powers that run the Lebanese American University—where I'm enrolled in this Arabic course, staying in their glitzy apartment (that's actually a dorm)—get so much business from the conservative Saudis and Gulf states that they have imposed these archaic Arabian rules around here: like no chicks & booze in the room, which is a major problem for nearly everyone here.

Most of the rich Saudis seem to get around this by bribing the "guard" in the lobby when they want to bring hookers up to the room. And every weekend they do. But the other option for getting around these rigid rules, the sly option, is The Gay Option. Why not? The blundering Arabs would never see it coming!

So like a queer genius, my "floor monitor" has his Special Friend come over every day after work . . . "Just coming to hang out," he'll say to the guard, and then he'll take the elevator up to the tenth floor and slam his apartment door closed.

Fuckin' genius, I think.

While my Saudi roommate from Mecca and I have to smuggle booze into our place like Al Capone, taking unchased pulls in our apartment, with no women, those fluffies next door have the time of their lives, humping like wild animals. And I should know . . . WE SHARE A WALL.

———

Sitting here, I can safely identify that the bummer of Beirut is twofold: there's no surf, and even if there was, the reef along the corniche (waterfront) doesn't seem like it'd take a good swell. Since I landed here with Che a few weeks ago, I've been going on afternoon jogs around the city. I really should reevaluate my exercise, because hardly a goddamn day goes by where I ever so narrowly miss getting slammed by some hysterical Lebanese cabbie, arms up in the air, crying like some hell-soul for everyone to clear the fuck out of his way. *But what the hell?* I don't have a car and I'm too afraid to ride a motor scooter, so jogging shall remain my way to explore the city. It's a good way. A cheap way. A way that up to This Very Instant hasn't gotten me killed . . . or as the locals say, a proven method for public safety.

My favorite running routine is to take the elevator down to the lobby and head south from my West Beirut dorm. I like going that way because I have befriended the Lebanese military guards who have set up a checkpoint, questioning every Tom, Dick, and Hussein who wants to pass along their street. So it's easy to see why a Grand Ayatollah in smartassery (me) would become friendly with these dudes. Their job is to basically wait around on the street and shoot back at whoever shoots at them first. So anything that takes them out of That Reality is an obvious relief.

Naturally, being young men with large guns, these army dudes are scary to the record-setting flocks of tourists who are in Beirut this summer from America, Saudi, the Gulf. But to the Lebanese, they are nothing more than a bunch of *pussies*, who couldn't even keep Hezbollah from marching into West Beirut in May 2008. Just the sight of a gringo six-footer in a beer drinker's tank top and running shorts seems to take these guys away from the heart attack of having to police the place . . . it's as if my perceived California character makes them Break Character. Good journalistic access, indeed.

As for these Lebanese checkpoint dudes themselves? Man! Talk about an impossible job! These dudes are tasked with trying to convince the brazen Lebanese people, who from 1975 to 1990 fought the goddamn civil war, personally, that they have control over the streets . . . like there aren't uncollected grenade launchers in *every* building that surrounds them. And to dwell on bummers, these checkpoint dudes don't even have any good weapons! Nothing like the Israelis (an utterance that is best not made around here). Just from jogging through, I've noted these soldiers have an automatic rifle, a uniform, a helmet, orders to provide security, a pisskop of an old armored personnel carrier to sleep in—all to be ushered out on a wing and a prayer, hoping to make it through That Day . . . or maybe just Today.

So it is in a sort of sick humor that I joke with these dudes. Sometimes, I bullshit them quite a bit. Once, I just lost it and told one of them I was a CIA spy. And always, when they let me through, I continue on my jog, breaking right at the corner—down a street filled with low-end brothels, a Donald Duck toy store, tall hotels, and the stale whiff of the SSNP headquarters. AKA, the Syrian Social Nationalist Party. Or as the SSNP brags on their website, "the thuggish brute of doomed Lebanon."

In Beirut the foreign press has a comfortable history of turning Hezbollah into a bogeyman . . . and really, why not? They're the only faction still armed from the civil war, with enough conventional firepower to overthrow the Lebanese state. But it should also be pointed out how much of a joke and underused the SSNP is . . . the pan-Arab Nazi admirers who would love nothing more than to claim the entire Levant, most of Iraq, and Cyprus (for some reason) and turn the area into some kind of Semitic Fascistdom called Greater Syria. But don't let *theory* trip you up. These are the same Lebanese thugs who gave the internationally acclaimed journalist Christopher Hitchens a hardened ass whoopin' on the famous Hamra Street in February 2009, when he scribbled "Fuck the SSNP" on their swastika-like sign. When ole Christopher was thoroughly beaten & bruised, and safe in the comforts of some Western hotel, he defended himself, saying, "Swastikas exist to be defamed." But Hitchens didn't just scribble on Any Sign . . .

. . . This Sign marked the site on the famous Hamra Street in West Beirut where an SSNP goon named Khalid Alwan decided to murder two Israeli soldiers for trying to pay for their lunch with Israeli shekels. The Israelis' paying in shekels infuriated Alwan beyond belief. I mean, the man just fucking snapped when he saw the Israelis try to pay with their money! Apparently, it was one thing for the Israelis to occupy the city, but another thing to disrespect. So the young Alwan took out a side arm and shot the two Israelis in the open café, launching what the necktie intellectuals refer to as "the escalation of Lebanese resistance."

———

So, on my jogs—my daily Beiruti surf check—I venture through the army dudes' checkpoint and pass by the much-feared SSNP headquarters. Every time, I think, *they can't all be thugs*. But they are. The Hells Angels of Beirut. The same grain-fed swine that pussyfooted along with Iranian-trained Hezbollah fighters when they took the streets of West Beirut in 2008. The SSNP crept along with Hezbollah and hung their thug-evoking red swastika-like flags all along the normally respected Hamra Street—and nobody had the balls to take them down, even after Hezbollah eventually pulled out of West Beirut. In fact, it took President Suleiman himself to order them to be "lowered."

But even now, when I walk just off Hamra to this strange Pizza Italian place I can never remember the name of, I see SSNP flags, sitting, waiting in the alleys for The Next Time. This is truly the work of Mafia. Even for me, someone who has no real "steak" in this Lebanese BBQ, this is unsettling. There are plenty of wonderful

Lebanese people that I meet every day here who just want to live a normal life, like my Arabic teacher.

Back on the Birthright Israel trip, I remember talking to an ex-Israeli commando who said something like, "I'd love to go to Beirut someday . . . just talk to the people. I'm sure they're all *normal*, whatever that means . . . and perhaps I could ask them *why* they let Hezbollah shoot rockets at us." A decent request by the commando. A valid request. And the people I meet every day here in West Beirut seem like the sort he would get a kick out of talking to. Funny thing is that it's been so long since a Jew came out of the closet in an Arab country that most dumb Arabs can't even define what they're against! (Even though there are small Jewish communities in many of the Arab countries.)

Just the other day, my Saudi roommate said, "I don't care about Israel . . . I just don't want to see them bull-dozing Palestinian homes on Al Jazeera anymore." But the comedy in this is that the commando would be *fine* walking around nearly anywhere in Muslim or Christian Beirut. As long as the commando wasn't in his green Israeli commando uniform, trying to buy cappuccino on Hamra Street with shekels . . . he'd be fine. Everyone would write him off as just another stumbling tourist, or some kind of Western hippy—probably Italian—in

Lebanon to take in the spice of it all . . . off tomorrow to the Roman ruins of Baalbek. Something the Italians consider Theirs. And hell, they built half the tourist industry in the Levant. The Roman ruins? If you drink enough wine with enough Italian tourists, you're bound to meet the Italian who drunkenly blurts out, "The Lebanese! They should be paying us for a tourist visa!" And then you walk the stumbling guido home as it will only be time until the Lebanese *mukhabarat*, or secret police, will be up both of your asses with a poker, brutishly working to excavate The Facts—just another precaution, reserved only for the weak in this city . . . Beirut. The powerless are nothing here.

———

But what am I saying? I should really wrap up this keystroking ejaculation. But it's hard to resist keeping this blog going as the electricity is still on in my apartment . . . it's impossible to get any goddamn work done around here as the power goes *out* not one, or two, or three, or four, or five, but six times a fucking day! Amazing. The Lebanese American University and my apartment are situated right next to the looking-to-be-confirmed Prime Minister Saad Hariri and his grand-ass palace in West Beirut. And the power *still* goes off six times a day! Does ole Saad (Hariri) not know this? Like I'll be drinking some smuggled arak with my Meccan roommate, enjoying him watch some bantering Islamist lunatic on the al-Manar TV station (the Hezbollah news outlet) and all of a sudden—*Zaap!*—the power goes! Why?

Are we not within the range of a three-wood drive from Saad Hariri's compound? Actually the gay floor monitor next door keeps telling me that Hariri has a generator, not to mention a frightening band of snipers scattered along his roof at all hours. The kid also says that the Lebanese American University got this building at a reduced price because nobody wants to live this close to Hariri . . .

"Why?" I once asked.

"Because a truck bomb killed his dad," said my flamboyant floor monitor, touching my arm in that way some gay men often do, "and it's only a matter of time until a truck bomb kills him."

So in other words . . . this screen I'm looking at, my Meccan roommate asleep in the next room, and everyone in this apartment building could taste the wrath of that inevitable truck bomb, as it will someday come crashing into Hariri's palace, just up the street. "And it will happen," continues the kid (still touching me) like I wasn't *mortified* by his truck-bomb comment the first time.

My Meccan roommate understands this fact: he's a jittery wreck (when he's watching TV) as every half hour he leans over the couch to open the window, puff the butt of a cigarette, and look around. The Meccan turns back from blowing smoke outside, and tells me he can't stop looking at the snipers along the roofs, like they're watching him through the scopes of their rifles. Why not? 5:45 isn't too early/late for those clowns.

And Hariri is a clown—born in Saudi Arabia to an Iraqi mother and educated in America, he's the rich playboy of West Beirut, vying to be the next prime minister of Lebanon. Hariri's biggest problem is that he lacks the chutzpah to be anything but a pro-Western politician. Without their support, American support, he is doomed. Hezbollah's secretary general, Hassan Nasrallah, on the other hand, Hariri's so-called opponent, now that's a man of charisma. My Meccan roommate is a devout Sunni from Mecca, for God's sake, and he *loves* watching Nasrallah (a heretic Shia) on TV. "He speaks to us," he says.

The Meccan's right: from the patchy *ayns* of Arabic sounds I'm starting to pick up, I can understand that Nasrallah isn't your standard Arab leader; he doesn't talk *at* the people, he talks *to* them. My Meccan roommate will hug his pillow on the couch, saying things like, "Look, Jesse, I think the Shia are going to hell for portraying people in Islam . . . but that Sayyed Hassan, he is *wonderful* . . . a good man—and he speaks *to us*, right here in this room!" And then there is Hariri, the lame subject of this paragraph who only really makes sense by contrast: whenever the Meccan and I watch him on TV, he comes off like a soft-spoken weakling who pays a bunch of supporters (and journalists, but not this one) to come into his fortress up the street and cheer for him as he plows through some pep-rally teleprompter, just beyond the camera's pan. Hariri's the kind of guy who doesn't seem like he's had to fight for anything in life. So just because Hariri's got a fancy facial trim and uses enough hair gel to count for economic stimulus doesn't make him fun to watch—or listen too. Or even follow.

———

But enough of that. What does it matter? I'd like to continue my study of Arabic here in Beirut, finish my journey of surfing from Israel to Lebanon, and perhaps even get a job out here. Then I could hunker down and write that article for the *Surfer's Journal* I came here to write. But I keep applying for jobs here in Beirut and coming up empty-handed. I've tried all the English newspapers—even a job at the British Embassy, thinking that if I swear allegiance to the Queen they'd take pity on my Yankee hide and brand me back into the Commonwealth. But no luck there, either. Goddamn recession! No jobs anywhere.

Very soon, I'm meeting the floor monitor's friend, Monner, a really cool American-Lebanese guy, to go surf this place in The South. (Monner is the floor monitor's "friend who surfs.") I don't know if there are going to be any waves this morning, but I just looked at my black & white cell phone that had a text from Monner: "Swell Cyps Good!" And what swell hits Cyprus, hits Lebanon. Even Israel. Perhaps the only thing that will cross the Israeli-Lebanese border today: surf. Perhaps the only thing the Haifa surfers and I will share today: surf. Probably the only reason I'm this adrenaline-ridden before the Lebanese dawn: surf.

And so we shall look for surf.

Monner can't get a car this morning so we are going to take a cab. He says he's "done it before" and he seems like a competent guy, so why not? I guess we'll see. Going this early is a good idea: the goons are still asleep; the military dudes down the street will be snuggled in their old armored personnel carrier; the rest of Lebanon's problems are snoozing; the wind is calm, or slightly off-shore. So we'll do it! We'll take a cab down to The South somewhere . . . figure it out!

Experience. Isn't *that* the meaning of this trip?

SURFING WITH NASRALLAH

Twenty years from now, you will be more disappointed by the things that you didn't do than by the ones you did do. So throw off the bowlines. Sail away from the safe harbor. Catch the trade winds in your sails. Explore. Dream. Discover.

MARK TWAIN

Wearing a backpack lined with random surf stuff, I carried Che down to the lobby of the Lebanese American University dorm. It was just past 6:00 a.m., the time I was going to meet Monner. And judging from the ruckus I heard on my way down, I was the only goon to consider this early hour to be morning rather than night. I stepped out of the elevator and looked around to see an open, white-floored lobby . . . but nobody in it. I walked over to the glass doors that made the entrance—but a metal gate had come down over them and barred the exit. *Damn. Locked. What now?*

I walked back into the lobby and noticed a night guard lying on one of the red couches. His shoes were off, his head was resting tenderly on his arm, and his hand was tucked like a baby's between his crossed feet. He was wearing a loosened red tie with a black suit and high-rise dress socks. If he hadn't been asleep on the job, looking downright hilarious with his creeping moustache smile, I might have just gone back to the gate and muscled the fucking thing open myself. But this was too amusing to walk away from. I paused, appreciating the humor.

"Sabah al-khair," I said, in a soft and questioning manner . . . it still seemed early and I wasn't keen on causing a scene with the asleep-on-the-job guard. The man sniffled a bit—his smile growing with pleasure and thoughts of hedonistic lust. Clearly, he was off on some hot Greek island with naked nymphs, and they were feeding him grapes and singing that wild song that once enticed Odysseus on his bumbling odyssey. In his dreams, he was far away from the heated streets of West Beirut—and the truck-bomb blast radius that we were currently within. Prime Minister–elect Saad Hariri's mansion was only a block away. And hazard pay was something only laughed at in Beirut.

"Hello?" I said, switching to English, now with a bit more force.

The guard jolted back to reality. He jumped up off the couch, away from the nymphs, and brushed himself with one quick swipe. Then he steamed toward the vault-like gate, as if he had been going through this pisser of a routine all night. He didn't even acknowledge that I had a surfboard and was going to surf at this ungodly hour. I guess he just didn't care—and he must have thought the same thing about the gate, because after I passed through, he didn't even lock it. He just walked back to the red couch, undoubtedly to dive back in with the naked nymphs.

Okay. I'm out on the early morning street . . . where is Monner?

In California, one of the most bummer things about going surfing in the early a.m.—when the wind is especially calm, making the water glassy and smooth—is that your friends are often "too tired" (hungover) to meet you at the announced spot, making your morning carousing with the sea a solo experience.

The night before I'd had this bothersome worry, whether Monner would show. But I got the feeling from him on the phone that he would be good for a morning session. Sometimes in life, you just have to trust your intuition.

"Jesse!" a voice yelled. "Down the block! Can you see me?"

Sure enough, there he was, maneuvering his surfboard into a cabbie's trunk, *carefully*—a worthy skill that marks the difference between a surfer and a frantic Middle Eastern cabbie. I walked over though the darkness of the Beiruti morning. We greeted with a California-ish hand slap and made a comment or two about nothing. Then Monner proceeded to tie Che *carefully* into the trunk.

This was a technique I had never used before. It seemed dangerous as it left half of our just-over-six-foot boards sticking out the back, making them vulnerable to escape, hijack, speed bumps, tailgaters, loose tie-ins, Israeli air strikes, and really any other looming hazard that makes up an ordinary morning in Lebanon.

But this was the genius of Monner: unlike your standard dumbass, Monner had thought through these issues. In his backpack, he'd brought a set of bungee cords that allowed us to strap our boards down and into this trunk with authority . . . thus eliminating escape, speed bumps, and loose straps from our list of potential morning disasters. As for hijack and tailgaters, the streets were nearly empty, with the exception of a few stumbling drunks coming back from whatever party (or brothel) they had been enjoying. As for the possibility of Israeli air strikes . . . well, I'm not quite sure how to end this sentence . . .

Whatever pre-dawn surprises were waiting for us, we were ready. I was itching to surf. Monner and I said little to each other in the cab. We both basked in the warm and epic feeling that we were up to something big.

Where we were going wasn't far south, but it was amazing how just leaving the fine streets of West Beirut and venturing out of the city could change the vibe. Things seemed more rural, unannounced, like we were entering a bucolic wilderness of smaller Lebanese towns. Israel and my dude-buddies in Haifa were getting closer by the mile. But of course that pesky goddamn closed border was in the way, with both Hezbollah and Israel guarding the place in a way that wasn't worth physically confirming.

Searching my head while riding in the cab, I realized I knew little about this Jiyeh place. It was just a foreign name to me. *Jiyeh.* Hard to pronounce. And it wasn't at all what I expected when we got there. *But what had I expected? A wilderness, with no establishments, and Biblical characters living in a nudist utopia?*

Without warning our cabbie jumped the highway and plowed down to a rustic frontage road. After a short distance, he again broke right and turned into some rural beach resort. *Was this Jiyeh?* It was still dark and too hard to make things out. We hadn't even seen a wave yet.

"Monner, dude, are you sure this is where we want to surf?"

He looked at me blankly. "Yeah! If there are waves, it'll be good." Monner handed the cabbie a crisp American twenty and in the dark we unstrapped our boards, still half-dangling out of the trunk. Without pause, the cabbie sped off, back in the direction of Beirut.

As we made our way through the deserted beachfront bar, I could make out open bottles of hard liquor and half-filled glasses from the night. The party seemed to have just ended. Near the edge of the deck, lounge chairs and cocktail tables came dimly into focus. I almost stumbled into a pool in the darkness, as the sounds of the sea were mostly guiding us.

At this dark hour, not a soul was around, and we both took a seat on the edge of the deck, our toes dangling off as a keen euphoria took hold of our under-slept minds.

Our first glance at the Sea.

The fine pre-dawn excellence in the air meant we had picked the right morning to come. By noon this place would be filled with all the plastically altered bodies known as "the young and wealthy of Lebanon." But that was no problem. By that time, the wind would have switched directions and ruined the align-ment of conditions that made this moment so serenely surfable.

I turned my head in the darkness and could make out that there was a small village surrounding this resort. Slices of the wild Lebanese coast could still be seen—beautiful, perhaps even unaltered since the days of the ancient Phoenicians.

"Wow!" Monner exclaimed. "It's not big, but what would you say, chest, shoulder high?"

Indeed, I thought, and nodded with gleeful approval. My stomach clenched with excitement.

The wind was not blowing in from the sea as it often did in the afternoon. It was coming in from up the wadi, hitting my face as if I were in a wind tunnel. This lush mountain air had been storming across the Asian continent and out to the end of the line. Crisp waves broke over the Jiyeh sandbars. Their crests rose, rooster-tailing with huge spray, and left the water smooth and clean and perfectly rideable for my first morning of Lebanese surfing.

The moment was here.

"Oh yeah!" I said in a whipped craze of almost-mission-accomplished adrenaline. "We gotta get out there!"

Barefoot, I jumped onto the grainy sand—as did Monner—and we started to wax the tops of our boards to give us grip. Monner was going to ride some kind of soft-top board, normally used for beginners, but it's all he had here in Lebanon, as there were no surf shops. The closest one across the forbidden border wouldn't be far, but venturing there was most definitely out of the question.

Waxing in a circular motion, I uttered that it was too bad I hadn't known him before or I would have gotten my buddy Lee to make him a board in Haifa.

"Yeah, that would have been great!" Monner said, while spreading an oozing glob of sunscreen all over his face, making it zinc-white. And again, there was the beauty of Monner: he wasn't big on Israel, but he wasn't even close to being so rigid as to not accept a board from an Israeli.

Looking out, I could see that the conditions were getting better. The sun was still hiding somewhere up the wind-blowing wadi, behind the mountain—as if the cool Asian air were actually making the difference in pushing that old fireball over the craggy peaks of ancient Phoenicia.

"Next time I'm in America," started Monner, "I'm going to get a fiberglass board like Che. Then I can really start surfing around here!"

I looked at Che with a warm sort of friendship, perhaps knowing that he could never leave Lebanon . . . for this was his intended destination all along. He was built for these waves, and it didn't seem right to part him from his journey, for he had also risked his foamy life to come here. It was too defining. Too important. He had passed through all the checkpoints and hassles that I had—minus the gassing at Bil'in—and our journey had really bound us together.

But we weren't there yet. With my toes in the sand and Che firmly tucked under my arm, I heard a fine-breaking set come crashing across the Jiyeh sandbars, peeling effortlessly without a soul out there to ride it. Monner and I knew the wonderful offshore wind—whiffing of the cedars of Lebanon—wasn't going to last forever. So just as Lee and I had done 55 miles south in Haifa, we hurled our adrenaline-ridden bodies off the sand and into the Jiyeh sea, like two old buddies who had known each other forever.

Finding a lull between sets, we enjoyed a smooth paddle to the outer calm of the break. It was then, as I sat upright on Che, that a strange feeling crept up my spine like a high that would never be felt again: Completion. Elation. Utter Sublime. The touch of God. A shooting star that proved Existence: I couldn't have been closer to making my dream a reality.

Being out in the Jiyeh break was an experience as radical as anything I had felt in the Middle East. Or anywhere, really. I was teetering on the finish. After all the hassles and planning for the better part of a year, I had figured out a way to surf on both sides of the Israeli-Lebanese border, and I had done it in a way that I could write about for the *Surfer's Journal*, my first job out of college.

But I had yet to catch a wave . . . and so it was just as the new day's sun rose above the tallest peak of the deep valley that a set of maritime mounds started to rise from the depths of the sea.

Monner and I were in position. He looked over at me with an expression that meant one thing only: *Go man! This is yours!*

Softening my upright position, I extended my legs straight and slid my belly down on Che's waxed deck. Cupping my hands, I reached forward to fully grasp the warm water and push it all the way through in long, powerful, strokes. I leaned left, position-ing myself right under the steepest part of the rapidly building peak. I knew I would only get one shot at making this first crest of completion—and my first Lebanese ride had to be worthy.

One paddle. Two paddle. Three!

I could feel the power of the wave pick me up, making my long strokes in the sea irrelevant, for a new force had taken over. Arching my back, gripping the rails, I planted my front foot down, twisting it, and crouched all the way through—down the line, enter-ing that sweet pocket that held me like a child, shepherding me through My First Ride, which could never be felt again.

I shrieked with joy. Monner was smiling with approval. I was in the calm periphery of the break, drenched with ecstasy and slowing down as all the elements had come together for a wave that was downright mind-bending. Those first moments of completion were the absolute zenith of the trip. I couldn't get any higher. I had fulfilled my desire to surf in the Middle East when I was in northern Israel. And now in Lebanon? Sweet Jesus! It was just great!

With all the odds stacked against me—both figuring out a way to get to the Middle East and surfing around the Israeli-Lebanese border—I did what I had set out to do. I felt like an old man at peace with a well-lived life; or like an old blues gui-tar player, wailing a heavy lick through a screen of distortion, who finds that last needed note and massages it elegantly for a sweet payoff.

That first Lebanese ride was the first time in my life I felt like I had completed something that made all the hassles and checkpoints and closed borders worth it. Like it had all come together. It was a feeling so rare and beautiful that who knows if I will ever feel it again?

Frankly, who cares?

———

Since Monner and I were the only surfers in the water, and Mediterranean surf doesn't have long periods in between sets, there was never the feeling that we were waiting for waves. More than often, I found myself feeling funny for letting a perfectly good, shoulder-high set of waves pass right under me. With all the nonstop surfing and paddling, we were getting some serious exercise. It was a wonderful feeling. But around 8:30 a.m. our paddling arms began to wear out. And an epic feeling of early-morning exhaustion took over.

"Yo, Monner!" I called, paddling over to where he sat resting on his board. "What about breakfast?"

My fair-skinned Lebanese friend grinned. "I know just the place!"

Feeling parched, Monner and I took the last wave all the way into the shore on our bellies. When we hit the sand, Monner walked up to his backpack and pulled out two water bottles to replenish what had so successfully been purged from our glands. Just like in Haifa. The salt of the sea.

We picked up our boards and backpacks and walked back through the empty resort and onto the frontage road that ran straight into the main village of Jiyeh. After about five minutes of walking, I spotted a most unusual thing.

"You see that?" I asked Monner.

"No—what is it?"

A car raced toward us down the open road, transforming from a mirage into a vehicle, and my suspicion was confirmed: That long, white thing strapped to the top of the car was a surfboard!

Monner and I both set our boards down and waved to the swerving car. Loud and clunky, the thing screeched to a stop about ten feet past where we were standing. A guy, who looked in his late 20s, got out of the car.

"Surfers!?" he gulped, in near-perfect English. "From where?"

"I'm from Tripoli . . . and also Beirut," replied Monner, also in near-perfect English.

"California," I said, wondering if it would be funny or not to say "Israel."

The lone surfer got out of his car and came right over to us to slap hands Hawaiian-style and introduce himself as Hassan. Here was a guy with a Billabong tank top who had clearly spent time in some English-speaking country (perhaps mine) looking for the same thing we were: surf. There was an instant connection along that deserted frontage road. Though I could sense there was a moment of *pause* between him and Monner. As in most random Lebanese encounters, I could sense each was trying to figure out the other's religion and kin. But it all seemed to go well. And they were speaking in English and talking about surfing, so feudal, go-fuck-yourself Lebanon would have been a stretch on that quiet little road.

Hassan explained, "I've been driving all morning and haven't found any good waves. I'm actually on my way back from Beirut now. I was down at the big yellow house in Sour earlier."

"The big house in Sour?" Monner asked, with a new-found interest.

"Yeah, you've never surfed there? It's probably the longest wave in the Mediterranean. Usually, you can ride it forever—thought it wasn't big enough today."

The Mediterranean did not normally produce big waves in the summer. Winter is almost always when the biggest surf hits. But what the hell? The thrill of the sport is so addicting a high that it's impossible *not* to get hopeful and sidetracked every once in a while. Next thing you know, you're off on some big adventure, finding yourself lost and chasing some haunting memory from the past. It's something every surfer can tell you about. And most don't even try to fight it.

As I smiled in recognition of Hassan's feeling, my eyes dropped to the yellow Hezbollah flag dangling from the keychain he was holding. *Now this is interesting.* It was either a smartass form of "surfer camouflage" that allowed him to move with ease through Hezbollah-controlled parts of the country, or he was an actual Shia Muslim and member of Hezbollah. Either way, this potentially "longest wave" was no more than 40 miles south from where we were standing, and very near the Israeli-Lebanese border.

"It's actually okay to go down there if you have a legitimate reason," Monner would tell me later. "Most people would understand surfing on the coast, but the South can be *very* different.

Actually, I've never been further south than Saida." And Saida was only nine miles south of where we were standing.

If Hassan was indeed a keychain-carrying member of Hezbollah, it would be significantly easier for him to get through checkpoints and deal with Hezbollah security than it would be for Monner, who was a half-American Sunni from a completely different part of the country. His grandfather was the founder of the Lebanese Communist Party, for Christ's sake—not an Iranian-trained ayatollah, but a secular intellectual, who wasn't a likely fan of bearded theism. So it would be much tougher for Monner to explain himself in that part of Lebanon.

But even then, Sour is less than 20 miles north of Israel and it's under constant watch. A simple thing, like parking on the side of the road to surf, would likely prompt a few questions from some Hezbollah internal security officer who just didn't grow up prowling the Lebanese coast for waves.

If Hassan wasn't a member of Hezbollah, he was a damn clever bastard, and I would have enjoyed his cunning front. Which seemed to be the ticket for this whole surfing the Middle East thing: whoever's turf you are surfing on, allow them to believe that your sympathies are undoubtedly with them; before the conversation even starts, the people with the power and guns can see that you are definitely not a threat. The secret with the surfboard was to get the potentially hostile person in charge to break character, whisking their mind away from the troubles of the Middle East . . . and spray them with a fresh breeze of California attitude, culture, and mirth.

We chatted with Hassan for a few minutes longer, urging the dude to just "jump on it" since the wind would soon be switching directions, blowing out the surf. We took his number. He took ours. And we shook hands again, agreeing that we should all surf together soon.

I never saw Hassan again. Though I'm sure he's still out . there . . . with his Hezbollah keychain, riding the waves near the big yellow house.

———

When I kick off my shoes and think back to my first day of Lebanese surfing, Jiyeh lives as something of a perfect spot for me. It was like an Eden of sorts. Yet as we walked along that frontage road to breakfast, Monner said the place had been unsurfable for years. Only recently had he started surfing it again, which made me curious about this seemingly all-wonderful place.

To the left of the sandbars, a few hundred yards from the break, a refinery rested at the tip of the half-moon bay that crested back out to sea. In the 2006 war, Israeli air strikes hit this refinery, causing an oil spill that seeped onto the Jiyeh shore and soaked the fine sandy beach with the dark hells of conflict.

On the other side of the Jiyeh break was another remnant of battle: an old, rusty boat, perhaps 40 feet long, sunk deep enough in the sand that it wasn't going to budge—which was fine because like most ruined things in Lebanon, nobody was going to move it. At one point while we were surfing that morning, I paddled over to the vessel and checked out its gutted cabin, to see if I could find a rusty old machine gun or something. Really, it just looked intensely cool from the surf line up and I wanted to check it out. So I paddled over to it, climbed aboard, and parked my surfboard on deck. I then performed a dive—mostly for Monner's amusement—with a highly botched back flip, slapping the Mediterranean with a boisterous splash that stung my back for a good long moment.

It is impossible to verify the actual history of a boat like this, since nearly everyone Monner and I talked to had a different story. But according to some of the owners of the beachfront resorts—and their slave-waged workers, whom we would meet on our return trips—this boat once belonged to "Palestinian arms smugglers." It had been shelled before their cache could reach the shore.

In Lebanon, there seemed to always be this pseudo-lie that sought to blame everything on the Palestinians for marching into Lebanon and eventually starting the civil war. And when that scapegoat failed, there was always another loathing Lebanese faction to blame: "Fuck the SSNP!" Or Israelis. Or whoever pissed you off during your morning coffee.

Regardless of whose boat it was, or how it got there, it had spent over 30 years rusting at the Jiyeh break. Later in my journey, while reading on top of some haggard old casbah in Aleppo, Syria, I stumbled upon a stomach-wrenching passage in Robert Fisk's *Pity the Nation*, telling how Druze militiamen ravaged the little town in 1985. When it was over, civilians were told that they would be compensated for the hundreds of homes that had been razed. That never happened—and the Maronite churches were dynamited and bulldozed to the goddamn ground.

This wasn't exactly the first thing I was thinking about that morning, especially after the elation of finally getting to surf in

Lebanon. But there it was, staring right back at me: those fine Jiyeh sandbars were triangulated by the refinery, the boat, and Jiyeh itself. That sleepy little town had more to it than just being a beautiful place with fine waves. It too had seen its fair share of the sickness that lurks along the Eastern Mediterranean. And while everything was fine at the moment I was there, who knew when the oils of war would again seep out of it?

Just like Lee, with his stories about random rocket fire, Jiyeh had a dark side. Without proper conditioning, it's easy to become exhausted by the emotional shift that comes with Middle East surfing . . . but maybe it's that very darkness that makes it so alluring in the first place.

———

Monner and I kept walking north along the overgrown frontage road that ran parallel to the sea. It felt tropical, as if the lush greenery from the wadi and the rolling escarpment of the southern Lebanese coast had all come together. In the distance, we could hear the grumble of trucks somewhere along the main highway, though it seemed far away.

Eventually, we came to a rural intersection of sorts, with a gas station surrounded by a bounty of humid brush and banana trees. On the other side of the street I saw a few house-like structures, one of which Monner said was the breakfast joint. On the far street corner were two huge political posters: one of Saad Hariri, and the other of Hassan Nasrallah . . . glaring at each other, not more than ten feet apart. The pro-Western Hariri had just become prime minister–elect of Lebanon, and Nasrallah, who led the opposition coalition, had lost in the recent Lebanese election. For months, Nasrallah had been blocking an easy formation of a Hariri government, and with the signs obviously facing in at each other, it didn't take a goddamn Ph.D. to understand that this was something of a contested intersection . . . if intersections are even capable of being contested.

Now, keep in mind that this wasn't the American system, where politicians argue openly in public, only to loosen their ties and have a cocktail and chat about it afterward. This was Lebanon. Where Saad Hariri's father, Prime Minister Rafiq Hariri, was assassinated back in 2005 when a massive truck bomb exploded just outside the St. Georges Hotel in Beirut. Many in the press assumed that Hezbollah had a finger in the operation. And to add to the tension, in May 2008, the Western-backed coalition cracked down on Hezbollah's telecommunications network, prompting Hezbollah fighters to invade Saad Hariri's stronghold in West Beirut. Members of the pro-Western government described the event as a "bloody coup," and were outraged that Hezbollah fighters would use their arms against Lebanese civilians and not the Israelis, whom they were meant for.

Pausing at this little intersection, smirking as this overwhelming history raced through my mind, I took Che out of his bag. I handed him to Monner and told him to walk over for a picture.

"What are the chances some fanatic will shoot us for posing with a surfboard in front of these guys?" I said, taking aim with my small camera.

Monner laughed.

That was another one of the truly great things about Monner: he never took any of the Crazy Lebanese Political Stuff too seriously. He knew that even though his country was plagued by seemingly never-ending sectarian violence and strife, the best way to fight it was with the Joke. In a sick, twisted, pig-fucker kind of way—that reminded me of how the Israelis joked about the Holocaust. I suppose it is also why "nigger" is so heavily pro-liferated in black rap music. Disarm the pain by engaging it.

"See that Lebanese army checkpoint over there? Nobody will do anything as long as they can see us." Unlike the army dudes I knew from my jogs in West Beirut, they seemed at ease in their rural checkpoint, sitting casually on their old trucks. Their rifles were down and I saw a few of them looking over at us with a baffled kind of amusement.

Monner stood there and I took the shot. Then we switched places. And no snipers took us out for our blatant smartassery.

Beyond the joke, I wanted a picture to remember the friction that existed so close to the waves we were surfing. There was a chilling feeling, as if the tension of Hariri and Nasrallah were looming like a blanket over the whole place, and nobody knew when the violence would flair next.

———

Lord only knows the real name of the quiet little hummus place next to the gas station at the turnoff for Jiyeh. Monner just called it The Hummus Place. When we sat down inside, I handed him some cash and told him to get me whatever he was getting—with double the amount of coffee for me. He smiled, turned on the balls of his feet, and walked out the front door, not saying a word.

Where the hell was he going? As my thoughts started to veer back to the possibilities of the intersection, Monner came strolling back in the door of The Humus Place. His California shorts and the smack of his flip-flops made him look wonderfully out of place.

"Where'd you go, man?"

Monner grinned. A minute later the butcher from next door walked in with two roasted lamb skewers, juices oozing out of them. *Genius,* I thought. It was fully okay to order a hummus plate with loads of strange vegetables that I had never seen before and supplement it with the roasting meats from next door. Why not? Then, a boiling pot of thick Arabic coffee came out with two small cups, and we dug into it all like wild beasts, clawing at one delicious thing after the next.

It was a long ride back to West Beirut. We opted *not* to take a cab on the highway, but a dumpy public bus—which ran along the frontage road and went through Beirut's southern suburbs, populated mostly with Hezbollah supporters, one of the hardest-hit targets in the 2006 war. Posters and pictures lined the road. Propaganda was everywhere. It was as if an old Joe Stalin had converted to Islam and designed the goddamn public display himself. Mock rockets were even set up in the centers of the roundabouts, aimed south, presumably at the fine surf in Haifa.

Looking out the window, it was clear that the Hezbollah supporters took pride in their armed struggle against what they saw as Israeli aggression in Lebanon. But what surprised me the most were the posters of Hassan Nasrallah, who came off as more of a warm grandpa you'd leave your kids with than the fiery secretary general of Hezbollah. Everywhere we looked, we saw signs of what Nasrallah called *muqawama*, or "resistance"—and they had built a whole society around it.

Feeling exhausted from writing my early-morning blog post and surfing at Jiyeh all morning, I spaced out in my seat. With the focus of my eyes growing soft, I could feel our bus bounce angrily along the surface streets and roundabouts. I gazed down at my flip-flops and remembered my first Lebanese experience with Hezbollah. Over two years ago. When we were all so young and foolish along the Eastern Mediterranean.

HEZBOLLAH DOWNTOWN

But really, I think of myself as a sensitive, intelligent
human being, but with the soul of a clown that always
forces me to blow it at the most crucial moments. (pull
of whiskey) I'm a fake hero. The joke the gods played
on me.

VAL KILMER AS JIM MORRISON, *The Doors*

The Beiruti street was wholly different in the summer of 2009 than it had been when I was there two years before. Literally, the opposite. In the spring of 2007, not even a year had passed since the 2006 war, and everything was still very much on edge in a shocked state of post-war bummer. There was no tourism. Beirut seemed gutted and deserted—like a hollow shell of its former self.

But that was actually okay with my two buddies (Jeffery and Jimmy) and me. When we touched down in 2007, we had no expectations and only a week off from our study abroad in Istanbul to get a taste. We knew it was going to be hot. Emotional. Even dangerous. But we wanted to know Lebanon for everything it was . . . and everything it wasn't. We wanted to see what travel writer Jan Morris once called the "impossible city." We wanted to discover ancient Phoenicia, the land of Canaan, the places of the Bible—though in a very secular kind of way. We wanted to explore the steamy nightclubs; the wild Islamists; and the crazed Lebanese, who were said to be "living way above their means." Simply, we wanted to be enchanted by whatever it was that had enticed us to buy tickets in the first place. I wanted to touch it.

Feel it. Let my eyes gaze upon it. Just not from the nest of my parents' TV room.

So it was one of those uneasy afternoons in 2007 on the open streets of East Beirut when the urge for drink came. We walked into a bar—a reggae hippy lounge thing with a few people in a few far corners. Twenty minutes later, I was enjoying a lusty chat with the sexy Lebanese-American bartender, who abruptly stopped and said, "Jesse, I'm a lesbian."

Well, goddamn! I thought. A possibility I had *not* pondered.

But it was she who first told me about BO18, and why the remaining Lebanese party hounds had left their once-inhabited downtown area.

This time, it wasn't because of Israeli air strikes.

———

BO18 was indeed the last place to party in the war-torn city in spring 2007. The 2006 war had sucked the economy out of Beirut and as a result, the downtown was a ghost town. Nothing was open. So BO18 held the buzz. It was an underground bunker on the periphery of the central party polis that was the last place for Lebanese sin; and as the lesbian bar mistress noted, the wild things didn't show till at least 2:00 a.m.

So after a few afternoon drinks and some low-end street falafels, Jeffery and Jimmy and I went back to our five-star Marriott suite for a nap. I had bargained our nightly rate at the place down to a considerable $30, as nearly all the fancy hotels in Beirut were vacant, some debating whether to just lock the doors altogether. (War-torn countries are a hell of a place to look for deals on high-end accommodations. In fact, I recommend it.)

And so it was somewhere after the clock hands bent around 2:20 a.m. that we arrived at the former civil war bunker known as BO18. We descended the concrete steps and felt the full bass of the music-bumping bunker abuse our souls. Two gruff men stood tall at the point of entry, in black leather jackets, patting everyone down for guns and collecting $20 for entry.

This was clearly a shelter for high-class spenders. Sexy, dark Lebanese women with sizeable breasts danced on tables. They wore tight jeans and elaborate designer tops. The men used hair gel like a drug—swooning and swaying to the hard beat of the club, they donned ostentatious sports coats over skintight T-shirts.

Jeffery, Jimmy, and I had slammed enough Drink at the Marriott that we needed nothing but a small, twenty-dollar iced drink to keep us moving. At one point, there was a small scuffle at the bar—but swiftly, big men in black blazers pounced to break it up. BO18 was a place for the most powerful of young Lebanese, and the owners weren't going to let the next civil war break out in Their Bunker. No former militia commander's daughter was getting her ass slapped by some opposing sect here. Money, power, family, and religion made a hell of an underground cocktail, and you could just light up and smoke the tension.

Every half hour or so, the roof would open, giving the steamy bunker a fresh blast of cool night air from the moonless sky. The three of us didn't know a soul and nobody wanted to associate with three budget-minded dumbass Americans on leave from their study abroad in Turkey. So we let the warmth of the alcohol guide us, grooving our bodies carefully to the pulsating beat of the club—taking in the experience of dancing with a level of wealth that most native-born Americans simply cannot fathom.

When the ceiling opened for the final time, the first beams of the new day's sun came crawling across the dance floor, as the end-of-the-night exodus was about to begin. We followed the crowd up the stairs into a parking lot filled with Ferraris and Hummers and other high-priced things. The taxi service that had brought us to BO18 a few hours earlier wanted triple the price for the ride back. So we just kept on walking, enjoying the early rays, blathering back and forth, trying to find the words for what we had just seen.

Eventually, Jeffery switched the subject. "How 'bout some breakfast?" he asked.

Jimmy and I agreed. It had indeed been a night of strong drink and experience, and with our money running low, cheap street falafel seemed like the next move. And so we kept moving, somewhere into East Beirut, occasionally getting glimpses of the early morning sea. In the distance I could hear the call to prayer from the Blue Mosque, meaning that we were nearing Martyrs' Square and the deserted downtown area we had been warned by the bar mistress to stay away from.

Still very much affected by drink, we approached a portable gate on the far side of the mosque. Jimmy blurted out, "What the fuck is this?" There seemed to be a makeshift city of portable tents and construction-looking things in the middle of the street that couldn't have appeared more different from the modern mosque and new buildings that surrounded it.

"Ahh, who the hell knows, man?" I said. "Probably a bunch of workers, fixing some blown civil war building or something." I suddenly flashed back to the first study abroad I did in junior college: Shandong University in Jinan, China, where just outside the university was a tent city that looked just like this blurry Beiruti scene. *Peasants from the countryside were shipped into the big cities to work like slaves!*

"It's just like China!" I proclaimed wildly to the guys. "I've seen this before."

———

Amid the towers of filthy shit-hole toilets, we entered the tent city. Though it wasn't for a good 50 yards that I sensed trouble.

Only a short time ago, my eyes had been fixed on the lifted tits of trendy Lebanese women. Those alluring images had now been replaced by posters of a strange, black-turbaned man with his right hand clenched in a raised fist. Sneering with lust, like a fiery cocktail of Ayatollah Khomeini and Che Guevara, there he was: Hassan Nasrallah. The Secretary General of The Party of God. Hezbollah . . .

Then it all clicked, why the lesbian bar mistress had told me to steer clear of the downtown area, and why the pro-Western elite were now exiled to BO18: over 3,000 Hezbollah-led protesters had camped in front of the parliament building, shutting down the economic hub that once fed the bustling streets of Beirut.

Having just put it all together, we giggled in a sort of horrified catharsis, as if the association of hard nightclub booze and anti-American rallies was some accident of publicity. Our little morning stumble had taken us into the Hezbollah protest camp that had brought Beirut to its knees.

THE KHAT EFFECT

A habit peculiar to the Yemenis is the chewing of a
mildly narcotic leaf called khat, mainly throughout the
afternoon . . . Addiction to the taste need not be feared.

THE BRITISH BANK OF THE MIDDLE EAST,
Business Profile Series

Since the tent city went up at the end of the 2006 war, Lebanon faced a period of menacing political unrest. The parliament, which hadn't met in 18 months, was in a state of crisis and couldn't agree on appointing the next president. Outside the Lebanese capital, this ineptitude seemed to raise the bar on political recklessness, and the people of Lebanon turned to their religious and ethnic sects for security and governance. In May 2008, General Michel Suleiman was nominated as president by the parliament; in no time, Lebanon became alive again, with the *New York Times* rating Beirut as the number one summer travel destination in 2009. It was crazy—as if people's perceptions just changed overnight.

In bars all across Beirut, journalists gathered deep into the night to try to make sense of what had happened. There was a strange sense that something was up, and it turned out that a grim character at one of these meetings had a most interesting explanation. According to comedian and journalist Nathan Hale, the Lebanese political crisis was the result of its leaders' getting addicted to an obscure stimulant not native to this part of the Middle East.

"Really," Hale once said over whiskey on ice, "if we all woke up tomorrow and saw the story that all the leaders in the Middle

East were secretly getting together and doing drugs, would anyone dispute it? Ha! In fact, it would explain everything!"

This was his take:

Beirut, August 2009 — Not much has been written about The Khat Effect as a serious factor in Lebanese politics, but as the third anniversary of the 2006 war approached—about a week before the rally—word leaked out that Hezbollah's secretary general, Hassan Nasrallah, was secretly meeting with the Israelis in hopes of acquiring some kind of strange drug. The Israelis, accordingly, were said to be Yemeni Jews.

For weeks it had been known that Prime Minister-elect Saad Hariri had been sneaking off to the Beqaa Valley for a performance-enhancing stimulant—as the fertile, Hezbollah-controlled valley is thought to be the center for the Lebanese drug trade. But it was tough to take the talk seriously until I saw Hariri on Al-Jazeera TV, struggling to find the strength to rouse even his most loyal fans. That was the key.

According to top Lebanese humanitarian and regarded earth scientist Samir Kuntar, the Levant is experiencing a severe drought, naturally affecting the supply of good Beqaa khat. "It makes it much harder to grow because it is not from here," Kuntar explains. "The lack of water combined with the election season is a worst-case scenario for the people of Beqaa . . . there is much demand but not enough water to keep up the purity of the crop."

But the man who felt this first was not Saad Hariri—though the Saudi-born, American-educated politician was clearly showing signs of cracking. The Beqaa Valley is also home to Hezbollah's logistics operations and is thought to be the secret residence of Hassan Nasrallah. Thus, it is entirely conceivable—given the known sickness of a wavering Beqaa junkie—that Sayyed Hassan was able to sideline his hatred for all Israelis, and meet very secretly with a small band of Yemeni Jews, in exchange for their indigenous stimulant, khat.

For hundreds of years the peoples of southern Arabia and East Africa had been growing khat—and in many instances, the drug was abused, as it was the popular "tool of the resistance" against that 1993 U.S.-led operation in Somalia that claimed many American lives. Sayyed Hassan has always been a keen student of international resistance, and it is more than likely that the "triumph of Somali militias" caught his attention. The only problem, as far as Sayyed Hassan was concerned, was getting the stuff for himself.

Fortunately for Sayyed Hassan, his archenemy, the Zionists, have spent the past hundred years bringing over

50,000 khat-chewing Yemeni Jews just below his base of operations in southern Lebanon. Apparently, with Hezbollah's help, these Jews have been snuck across the Israeli Line of Withdrawal, or Blue Line, that since 2000 has divided Israel from Lebanon.

Without doubt, a fresh-leaved mouthful of Yemeni khat would alleviate all sickness for Sayyed Hassan, and would give him just the boost he craves for this week's rally in south Beirut.

Unfortunately, the Hezbollah office in south Beirut has stayed quiet on this issue, giving "No comment" as their official response. (However, it should also be noted that they did not make any effort to deny these claims.)

In less than a week, all eyes will be on Sayyed Hassan as he gives his formal speech in the August 14 rally to "remember the martyrs of the 2006 war." It will be the intent of this journalist to observe the speech in an attempt to confirm some of the more eccentric side effects of The Khat Effect. Such symptoms include the waving of hands, yelling, and a highly hostile anger that is the marking of a fiending khat junkie.

"OUR ROCKETS CAN HIT TEL AVIV"

There was only one catch and that was Catch-22, which specified that a concern for one's own safety in the face of dangers that were real and immediate was the process of a rational mind.

JOSEPH HELLER, *Catch-22*

Brisking my three-week moustache for the last time, I lowered my head and continued down the dark alley toward the lights. I had gotten back to Beirut with Monner over a week ago. Now I was with two cats—Yusuf to my right, Nicholas to my left. We were white Americans, in our mid-20s, and we were walking buck-speed into a Hezbollah rally in the south Beirut district of Dahiya. It was nothing like the movies.

"It's like the cab driver said, guys," said Nicholas, maintaining his grueling pace. "No speaking English . . . with our dress and facial hair, we should look sort of Lebanese. In the darkness, we should at least blend in."

His words were encouraging, but like big-wave surfers, nobody ponders getting caught inside. The stakes were too high—a 100 percent commitment was needed here—for second-guessing or breaking from character. We were sliding down the crest of this wave, so we had to stay focused and allow our energy to melt into the vibrations of the scene. We needed to learn the Islamist beat that was growing stronger as we approached the massive open-air rally ahead of us. Into the unknown.

But the more I tried to submit to the rhythm the more I

thought about that all-so-famous civil war headline, "Hezbollah Captures Americans." And we were going straight into their lair.

"Stay close," Nicholas said, leading the way. "If anyone asks, we are here to pay our respects to the dead Lebanese from the 2006 war. How could they argue? And if they want us to leave, then we'll just do so." Nicholas looked at me, twisting in crazed laughter. "And you, Jesse, don't say a goddamn thing, you fucking Jew—this isn't a fundraiser for Birthright Israel!"

———

Hezbollah was definitely in control here. No Lebanese flag with its lonely cedar tree, no army checkpoint dudes, only Hezbollah. And all the complexities that made the Lebanese group so much more than just a junta militia: a family of five in one direction, a pack of teenagers in Western denim in another, the smell of fresh concession, men serving food and soft drinks. Everything ran All-Thick and All-Together with the pulse of the night, and into the tempo that binds The Party. This Party. The Party of God—Hezbollah.

The crowd was packed even tighter—shoulder to shoulder. Men everywhere were wearing articles of yellow Hezbollah clothing and long formal slacks. No women to be seen. They were on the other side of the rally, in the Female Section. This was an Islamist rally that sought a "moral standard," not to be confused with some kind of "immoral" dating scheme—as the conservatives often judge the mixed-gender events. Nobody was going to get a date while remembering the slain martyrs from the 2006 war. Hezbollah was going to make sure of that.

We approached a guard standing next to a big metal gate: he was tall, dark, and bearded like a devout Muslim, wearing a short-brimmed hat and black uniform. He motioned for me to "spread 'em" for a brisk pat-down. Done. Proving nothing was concealed in my crotch. Nicholas and Yusuf were behind me. They passed with a similar kind of ease. *Had the hairy brute not known we were American? What "Hezbollah" were we dealing with here?*

———

My pal Yusuf was a tall, white-skinned East Coaster in his mid-20s. I had met the guy in the summer of 2007, on a curb outside the Cave of the Patriarchs (the tomb of Abraham) in the West Bank city of Hebron. One of the Israeli soldiers guarding the perimeter said we weren't allowed into the Islamic side until after prayer was over—unless, of course, we were Muslims.

Without missing a beat, Yusuf walked up to the armed Israeli who guarded the entrance and said, "I am Muslim." Then they chatted piously for a moment—apparently convincing that Jewish sucker that he was a Muslim—and entered the mosque, without a backward glance.

I spent the next ten minutes on the curb immensely bothered, trying to figure out how I could piece together enough detail on Islam to dupe that Hebrew into thinking that I was also some kind of white Muslim. But I couldn't even work up the blinding confidence to try.

Only later, after I made a bitter comment to Yusuf about how he was only rubbing it in by making us all call him "Yusuf" instead of "Joseph," did he correct me: "Dude! I really am a

Muslim. *Islamic.* I converted a few years ago."

And now, a few years later, we had met back up in the Middle East and found ourselves trying to sneak into a Hezbollah rally. On my end, it seemed like a good idea to have a friend who was a follower of Islam at an Islamist rally. "Just paying respects," he could say to anyone irked by our presence. In the eyes of Hezbollah, being a Muslim would actually have been a convincing reason for our being there . . . it could calculate into their thinking.

On the contrary, it would have been hard to get past the prickly fact that our State Department deemed Hezbollah a "terrorist organization"; it surely would have pissed off that tall, bearded Hezbollah guard, who was definitely not friendly. So perhaps the only thing going for us was that 1.5 Yanks in our trio were Muslim. (Indeed, Nicholas was thinking about converting.)

But what about me? I wasn't thinking about becoming a Muslim . . . not even close. If I was caught, Che would be confiscated and sent to one of the many Hezbollah museums, lined with columns of blown-up Israeli tanks, where I would be forced to give tours of the goddamn place. I'd probably get sodomized by some wild ayatollah and sent off on some kind of savage khat reconnaissance mission deep into Israeli territory. "It's the only khat fit for our leader," the security official would say. Hezbollah rallies are no place for American Birthrighters.

———

We soon made our way through the surrounding buildings and into a massive public space that was going to be ground zero for the rally. All around, crumbled rock was dangling from the tops of the massive apartment buildings. Air strikes had destroyed them. But Dahiya was more than just another place to see blown-up buildings from the 2006 war.

At some point in the history of air strikes in Lebanon, the "Dahiya Doctrine" became something of a popular term in Israeli defense circles. It describes the tactic of blowing the sweet hell out of a hostile enemy, striking at the core of a guerrilla force whose armed infrastructure is hidden in its loyal civilian population. So the doctrine is asymmetrical: Israeli jets strike at the militia hard, and at urban areas even harder. They seek to exploit Hezbollah's most vulnerable weakness: its people.

Thus, Dahiya itself is proof that the Israelis believe in the concept of "kinetic deterrence." Hezbollah hides weapons within the very same apartment building that holds the families and children and everything precious to the Shia Lebanese. And so when the Israelis go—or are forced to go—on the offensive they often blow it all up together, like in Operation Cast Lead in Gaza.

High civilian casualties are very much a part of this type of conflict. That's what we seem to have such a hard time understanding in the West: Israeli-Hezbollah entanglements are very much about targeting "innocent civilians."

The Israelis wanted to make everyone who supported Hezbollah pay—by blowing up buildings, bridges, and roads—in an attempt to wean the population from the milky tit of The Party.

And just as for the Israelis, it was all strategy for Hezbollah. After the war, the goal was to leave some of these buildings for effect, rebuilding the rest in a populist image with lots of Iranian money. Hezbollah had to be *seen* by their Shia supporters (the civilian population) as indispensable; the last and only guardian for the downtrodden Shia—the hope in a hopeless state of BO18 lush children.

———

When we sit on our comfortable couches in the West and intellectually ponder the difference between Sunnis and Shias, we often think of the Irish and the difference between Protestants and Catholics: communities of theological difference, though everyone still basically drinks from the same pint. But in Lebanon—and in many cases across the Muslim world—the difference between Sunnis and Shias is also seen in culture and politics. In Lebanon in particular, tensions are inflamed by the governmental system—where each sect is appointed different access to political power, reinforcing sectarian identity and taking away from the sense of being Lebanese.

Today the Shia represent about 10 percent of the Islamic world. They have historically enjoyed influence, most notably with the Abbasid Caliphate and in Safavid Persia. Throughout the history of Islam, the Shia have been treated like second-class Muslims, often called heretics and subjected to persecution by their Sunni counterparts. In 1926, the French formed the Lebanese Republic, and nothing changed for the downtrodden Lebanese Shia—they continued to feel like underdogs all the way up until 1970, when the PLO was kicked out of Jordan and came with vehemence into southern Lebanon. Yasser Arafat's Fatah movement worked to build up their "resistance capabilities," asserting that it was the PLO's right to fight the Israelis from southern Lebanon. They created a state within a state—and with over 400,000 Palestinian exiles already living in the horrid refugee camps, the tiny Lebanese state was boiling with disaster.

In 1978, the Israelis invaded to crush the PLO. In 1981, the Israelis bombed the PLO. In 1982, the Israelis invaded again, moving all the way into Beirut—and it was said that Shia women in South Lebanon greeted the Israelis with flower petals. Apparently, living with the PLO was just that bad.

So it was somewhere in the late seventies, when everyone with the right stuff was experimenting, that the Iranian-born Shia named Musa al-Sadr came to the southern Lebanese city of Sour. He demanded that the Christians in Beirut give up some of their power; he wanted to give the Shia community a voice in Lebanese affairs. He openly accused the PLO of endangering Lebanese civilians in their fight against Israel.

Nearly all Shia Lebanese today remember Musa al-Sadr as the first modern figure who stood up for their community. He is also credited among many Iranian clerics as being the first Shia to surf the rich reef just beyond the waterfront in Sour. He was said to be a long-boarder—with a fine penchant for riding the nose.

———

In the football-sized dirt court of the rally, I was surrounded by massive apartment buildings: all white, facing inward, and per-haps a towering 12 stories high. On every balcony I saw family, friends, supporters—the very people thrashed by the 2006 war, showing up to say, "We felt it, too . . . but we are still here to sup-port you, Hezbollah."

There were thousands of white folding chairs, in hundreds of rows, and there were definitely going to be enough of them. People were hanging from the buildings, like jeering fans at a stadium. All their energy was focused on the Roman-style pillars that surrounded the stage, bellowing like some kind of Wagner-like *Apocalypse Now* monger, whipping everyone into a perverted frenzy.

All the flags of the big supporters of the Hezbollah-led March 8 coalition were waving: Amal, SSNP, Free Patriotic Movement, and Hezbollah. Which was interesting, because Hezbollah was supposed to be an Islamist party. Yet their Christian supporters showed up, waving their flags. *Was this not a closed Islamist rally?* Hezbollah wanted all sorts of Lebanese support, not just from their wholly Islamic Shia followers.

When I looked over at Yusuf, his eyebrows were raised in a sort of larger-than-life disbelief as the music and crowd and mania all jeered on. We passed by concession stands on the right of the massive court. We continued, into the ocean of white chairs. We took seats somewhere in the middle, so as to avoid being too close to the Hezbollah security guards, who kept moving with AK-47s along the perimeter of the chairs.

With the Wagnerian tune still piercing, a group of male teenagers filled in behind us, standing, cheering, and taking pictures of the front stage and each other with their camera phones. Yusuf, Nick, and I were stiff in our chairs.

To the left of our seated trio, an older Lebanese man shuffled in and sat right next to me, opening his callused palm, saying hello with a firm tap on my leg. I nodded—but made no eye contact. I didn't want to give too much energy his way. I didn't want to leak my feral "surferness." Not here. We couldn't afford to get outed, even if our presence wasn't a big deal.

The old man turned to me and said something, and I dropped my camera. I had been snapping stealthy pictures and videos. I picked out a word or two of Arabic from his pious sentence. I got the feeling from his aura that he was anti-technology. His slow and deliberate twirling of green Islamic prayer beads reinforced that I had to be on my best behavior—no casual contact or jokes. This old man wasn't just a Hezbollah supporter but an actual believer . . . alive and well when Hezbollah allegedly captured Americans. Maybe he had even been in on it!

Suddenly, the music stopped. Fireworks came screaming through the night sky, bellowing through the towering apartment buildings, which echoed an explosive boom. On the main stage, a massive movie screen came on, lit with none other than Sayyed Sheik Hassan Nasrallah. The man himself! Everyone was on their feet in ecstasy.

"*As-Salam Aleichem,*" said Nasrallah.

"*Walaikum As-Salam,*" replied the crowd.

It was unlike any speech I had ever seen by an Arab politician. Everyone was at ease—not scared—but feeling an absolute sense of elation and enthrallment. It was as if Sayyed Hassan was talking to them *personally*—as my Meccan roommate back in West Beirut liked to point out while watching him on al-Manar TV. His charming old-man quality was in overdrive—his bushy gray beard and red-faced smile were all the crowd wanted.

Then Sayyed Hassan shifted from his traditional, pan-Islamic greeting into a kind of colloquial Lebanese Arabic, knowing damn well that everyone across the Arab world was watching.

Even the Israelis were watching. Everybody wanted to know what the leader of Hezbollah was going to say on the anniversary of the 2006 war. *More rockets? And when?*

Just as I was starting to regret not spending more time learning Arabic, Nasrallah stabbed the air with his hand. And all at once, the crowd roared!

Yusuf whispered in my ear. "He's saying something about *muqawama* weapons and the greater resistance."

It was just what the crowd wanted to hear.

Then, abruptly, the satellite feed cut out . . . and he was gone. On the big screen now were faces and names from the front row of the rally. Famous Lebanese leaders were in attendance and tensely stood as their names were called: Walid Jumblatt, the Druze leader and head of the Progressive Socialist Party (some cheered); Prime Minister–Elect Saad Hariri of the Future Movement (everyone booed); General Michel Suleiman, the president of Lebanon . . . the list kept going.

Some continued to cheer as the names kept coming, but most still seemed bothered from hearing "Hariri." The teenagers behind me were especially irked. Hariri's name is not a good thing to blare over the speakers at a Hezbollah rally—he's the Sunni playboy from West Beirut who spends his money like a Saudi and doesn't know a goddamn thing about the suffering and humiliation of the poor Shia. That's what they think.

Everyone was riotous and worked up, grinding their teeth on their bitterness for Hariri . . . I could feel the tension brewing in the neighboring buildings and porches and through the sea of fold-out seats. The kids behind us were going crazy.

With the crowd in near revolt, the introductions ceased

abruptly and the movie screen went blank again. That was when Nasrallah showed his true brilliance—for he knew his Hezbollah brothers would react this way. And he knew just how to handle it.

His face came bursting back onto the screen, smiling. Dropping back into colloquial Arabic, he said, "And for you, Prime Minister Binyamin Netanyahu . . . *As-Salam Aluakum!*"

In an instant, the bitterness was replaced by laughter and total euphoria . . . and a touch of the surreal.

This cleric had come armed with jokes! He had addressed the Islamic world, the Arab world, his Lebanese supporters (and non-supporters), and now, Sayyed Sheik Hassan Nasrallah had just officially told the guy he shot rockets at to go fuck himself.

That scoundrel! And the crowd loved him for it!

Everyone was back under the spell of His Charisma.

———

At the end of the rally, we stood and made our way through the crowd and through the alley by which we had come. Out on the street were swerving sets of Hezbollah riders, two per bike, all with the guy on the back unleashing bursts from a Kalashnikov. From the curb, we hailed a taxi, and we headed back to the Duke of Wellington in West Beirut. It was mad craziness what we had done, and I was beyond-God thankful that I didn't end up captured and on the Internet, begging America to cut off its military support to Israel.

When we got to the Duke, I quickly pushed Nicholas and Yusuf in for a drink. We sat up high on our stools. The boys ordered virgin Shirley Temples (for Islamic reasons), while I got one of those big beers my Arabic teacher liked to drink (for non-Islamic ones). On the stool next to me was a fat, middle-aged Lebanese man, dressed in a fine suit, looking like the modern kind of Arab who wouldn't be caught dead at some mutinous Hezbollah rally. He said he was a professor, and you could tell he thought he was above their half-animal breed.

Sitting proud and high, like a dictator's diplomat, the fat man moved closer, crunching his cocktail in a way that said he'd clearly done it before. "The rally tonight? Yes, I heard . . . but they wouldn't let me in with this." He raised his drink in the air with a highly mocking, moustached grin.

"Well, you should have come with us, man." I said, jiving back. I reached down for my small camera, and skipped ahead to show him the fiery section of Nasrallah's speech.

The deep brows of the fat man rose, as he unconsciously started translating. "If Israel thinks it can destroy Hezbollah, then we are prepared to drop a bomb on any city in Israel . . . our rockets can hit Tel Aviv!"

The fat man broke into deep laughter. By now Yusuf and Nicholas were hunched over my shoulders, watching as Nasrallah was still shouting and waving his hysterical hand. The Khat Effect was now all but confirmed.

Hearing something, I glanced up . . . and to my amazement saw two scantily dressed hookers caressing down both sides of the fat man. My eyes peered straight into his: an unruly guffaw of "What the fuck?" came bursting from his belly as we could still hear Nasrallah wailing like a junkie in the background. The fat man grinned, slapped a bill down on the bar for all our drinks, and fondled the hookers all the way out of the Duke. Clearly, we were out of the Shia slums and back in Hariri's slice of West Beirut.

It was hot and crowded that summer along the Eastern Mediterranean, but there was always something to do when the surf fell flat.

And it most certainly had Edge.

THE VALLEY OF THE JEWS

All things are mortal but the Jew; all other forces pass,
but he remains. What is the secret of his immortality?

MARK TWAIN

A few weeks after Monner and I first hit Jiyeh, I picked up an English version of the Lebanese paper the *Daily Star*. The surf was again in one of those funky flat spells, Monner had gone back to the northern Lebanese city of Tripoli, and my Arabic course had grown to be frustrating—so digging through Beirut's longest-standing English paper at a coffee shop on Hamra Street seemed to be the call. I had now officially surfed in Lebanon, and while my eyes stayed glued to the surf report, I had this desire to see more of Beirut. I was in one of those beautiful moments of traveler's funk, off the high of my first morning of Lebanese surf, waiting for the next swell, trying to figure out the next seemingly random set of events in my life.

With surfing and the Hezbollah rally in Dahiya both within such close proximity to my apartment in West Beirut, I felt like there was no place I couldn't go. It was mind-boggling how fast I could get into a wholly new situation, a characteristic of Lebanon that reflects its depth and diversity. There are few other places in the world with such contrasts, especially in such an absurdly small space.

Whenever I travel, the best payoffs seem to come from quieting my thoughts and staying open enough to detect which previously locked door has decided to unlock itself. Prejudgment—and not judgment itself—is what defeats us. You never know what will happen unless you thrust yourself into the world. How can you know your full potential until you tune in to that lurking wave on the horizon? But you've gotta paddle out! All waves are hard to see when you're just standing onshore.

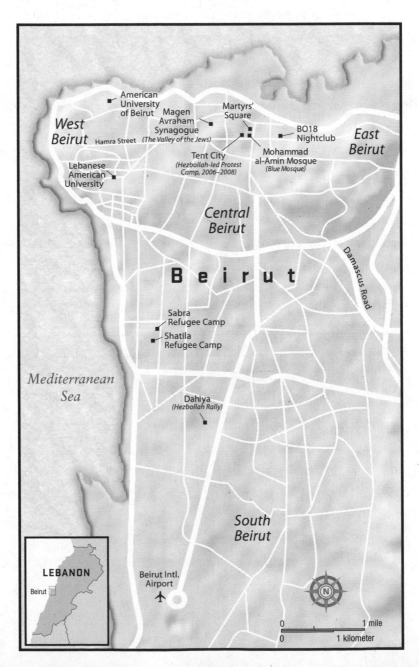

Buried somewhere in the back pages, amidst the plethora of various lifestyle pieces the editors decided was appropriate for the largest tourist season on record, was a story about Beirut's only synagogue. And there was the picture: standing just as tall as it ever had, with a slanted black iron gate, broken windows, and green vines wandering in, looking like some kind of Semitic Addams Family house gone greatly awry. It was quite the picture. And in the background was another one of Saad Hariri's famous Beiruti mansions; towering in all its high-priced Sunni Muslim glory, looking all the more glorious as its view alone seemed destabilizing to the wavering Jewish house of worship. Every piece of me confirmed my gut reaction: I wanted to go. *Experience.*

So I went back to my dorm room at the Lebanese American University and sure enough, my Meccan roommate—a small Saudi kid who was on the seventh year of his bachelor's degree— was watching Hassan Nasrallah's speech from a few nights before. I burst in, taking the Meccan's attention away from the wailing, black-turbaned cleric.

"Hey, man, look at this picture!"

The Meccan was barefoot; wearing loosely buttoned jeans, he couldn't have been more casual on the lavish red sofa. He ever so lazily leaned up and, a moment later, took the folded newspaper from my hand. "Ahh, yes!" he said, dragging out each word as if not to waste a cent of energy by speaking too fast. "Some friend has told me about this place." Then the Meccan set the paper on the sofa-side table and lowered his full weight back into the meekness of the cushion.

I protested. "Dude! We gotta go! Look how cool this thing is! It says in the article that it was ransacked in the civil war, that

Islamists looted it and even stole the damn Torah!"

But the Meccan was already back into the TV—with the channel switched to some white-clothed cleric on Al Jazeera now, ranting about the need to deliver a Holocaust to the world's "swine population."

"Goddammit! We're going!"

"Jesse. Please. We cannot go!"

"We're going! I'm calling Columb the Brit. And we're going!"

"No." The Meccan laughed nervously. "Let's just wait till they fix it."

"The paper says it won't be done till late 2011! And you live in Mecca, Saudi Arabia, for God's sake! When are you ever going to see a synagogue again?"

I really was growing to like the Meccan. He was the kind of kid who had never fully left the comforts of his lush Arabian oasis, but unlike the rest of the scoundrel *khaleges* (Arabs from the Gulf or Saudi Arabia) I knew in Beirut, the Meccan had a surprisingly modest, non–rich kid thing about him; and I knew that by playing into his Arab hospitality, he'd feel obligated to make sure I didn't get myself killed on some wild-ass adventure.

"Okay, Jesse! I'll go!" Then he proceeded to wave his finger like the ranting, anti-swine Islamist on TV. "But I'm not going to step one foot inside that Jeeeeeeeewwwww house!"

———

Say what you will about Saad Hariri—and I've certainly leveled a few "points of conjecture" at the man—but he does have a vision for Lebanon. Hariri is the guy who dreams of a secure, pluralist, and democratic Lebanon that embraces America. His vision is of a Lebanon that is united by tourism and the economic fruits that come with big business and government stability; and perhaps of most interest to pro-Israel American policy makers, he probably seeks a nonaggression pact, if not a peace treaty, with Israel. Hezbollah and the rest of "the resistance" are the obvious hindrances to this vision.

For Hariri, the extravagant downtown area of Beirut is the centerpiece for his plan. It is where he often lives and where he pours much of his personal investment. And somehow, Hariri's grand plan to turn Lebanon into an economic hub of tourism and commerce included the restoration of Wadi Abu Jamil ("The Valley of the Jews"), a small synagogue in the downtown area.

And so we loosen our ties and light up a smoke as we ponder that while Europeans were still persecuting Jews, Middle Eastern Jews enjoyed a quiet period of plain old living. Slight oversimplification, I know. But there were none of the pogroms or pitch-forkings that my Jewish great grandfather described when he escaped from that snake pit of czarist Russia. For the most part, the Jewish people lived as people with the rest of the people in a larger utopia known to academics as Peopledom. There was a level of integration into society then that today has all but left the land. Ask any Arab or Persian from the older generations about their childhood experience with Jews. Most, but not all, will tell you how they handled the money and were the only doctors their parents would go to when they were sick. They trusted them as a minority, and they were part of the integrated community.

In the 1960s, it was estimated by Isaac Arazi, a leading member of the Lebanese Jewish Diaspora community, that there were as many as 22,000 Jews living in Lebanon. Today, there are thought to be fewer than 100—and they have changed their names and converted to different religions and live deeper in the closet than those men with hats in the Catholic Church (which is ironic, because nearly all of the Jews in Lebanon are Sephardic, and their ancestors moved from Catholic Spain to flee the Inquisition).

There are thought to be under 2,000 Lebanese Jews left in the world today. Some live in Canada. Some in the United States. Some in Israel. And it was their money—along with some from Hariri and a loose collection of multi-faith Lebanese donors— that funded the $1.3 million it would take to fully restore the downtown synagogue, The Valley of the Jews. When it opened in late 2011, it was a place—in theory—for Jews to come back to worship. But for Hariri and his vision for Lebanon, the restoration of the synagogue—and its survival—will be a true test of his plan for the future.

———

Peeking around the corner of the famous downtown Beirut clock tower, I said to the Meccan, "So where is this 'House of Jeeeewww?'"

The Meccan scolded me with a look. In our short time living in West Beirut together, he had gotten to know my smartassery. And well. I had dragged both him and our British friend Columb from West Beirut in a flat-rate shared taxi, and we were now prowling for the synagogue in the downtown area. But it was hard to find; we only had the creased newspaper picture to guide us.

Our theory for finding it was easy: Hariri's mansion in the background, the haggard synagogue in the foreground. But the problem was that the architecture was all the same. All of downtown looked like Hariri's mansion. *Fuck! Which way?*

It was only after Columb the Brit and I pushed him a bit that we got the Meccan to ask the Lebanese guards near the clock tower for directions. The Meccan claimed he loathed speaking to random Lebanese people because they would quickly pick up on his Saudi dialect and assume he had come for the prostitutes, liquor, and fine Beqaa hashish, like so many Saudis before him. But the Meccan was free from vice, and he resented the trip that the Lebanese would lay on him.

Sure enough, as soon as he started talking, the guards looked at him very suspiciously. Columb and I laughed. The Meccan was right—they did treat him like a deviant Saudi hedonist who somehow escaped from Arabia. He came back with his head slightly down.

"Jesse, I still don't know why you want to go . . . you have a picture of this in your paper to look at."

I cut him off. "Where's the goddamn Jew house!?!"

"Okay. Okay!" snapped the Meccan, getting doubly defensive from the Lebanese guards and my impatience. "They said it was down here." He cringed, and looked right at me: "The Valley of the Jews."

We left the clock tower and meandered southeast as the Lebanese guards had advised. The buildings in this part of Beirut were all rebuilt—from government buildings to twenty-dollar-a-cocktail lounges to various embassies sprinkled on all sides. The coordinated architecture mixed the French influence of

Lebanon's past with this neo-Arabian thing. Sand-colored bricks were stacked high, warm and rich in the ancient rays of the Mediterranean sun.

At some point I noticed we were walking on a slightly downhill slope, and then, the sidewalk just stopped. Standing on the southeastern corner of a vacant intersection, it was clear that this civil war layer had yet to be absorbed into Hariri's downtown plan. We stepped off the cement onto the decades-old rubble of tangled and blown-up matter. Up ahead was a completely demolished building, blown up by some piece of artillery back in the dark days of Beirut.

The street sloped some more, and within the next city block I could see the assassination site of Rafiq Hariri (Saad's father) next to the famous Saint Georges Yacht Club and Marina on the sea. Across the street were the Phoenicia Hotel and the Holiday Inn. The blown-up Holiday Inn sat inconveniently on the Green Line, splitting Christian East Beirut from Muslim West Beirut. In the civil war era, militias tried to conquer the tower and send their snipers straight to the top, as they could fire on districts as far as Hamra and Ashrafieh from this elevated position in the heart of the capital.

Columb the Brit had already gone around on the dirt and was standing on the ruined side of the slope. When he glanced back at me, he cried, "Jesse, mate! Don't step a step further!"

Suddenly, I felt the rubble give a bit. I stopped, looked down, and realized I was standing on the half-leveled remains of a blown-up roof.

Holding my breath, I gingerly twisted myself on the balls of my feet and crept back onto the cement sidewalk. From there, I paced down and around the rubble on the dirt and stood shoulder to shoulder with Columb the Brit. We both let out a sigh of relief, agreeing that the thing looked a hell of a lot more dangerous from this side of the slope.

———

It was strange (and sinister) how much I enjoyed making the Meccan ask random Lebanese strangers where The Valley of the Jews was located. It made him so uncomfortable. The very reason he didn't want to go on Jesse's Crazy Goddamn Jew Adventure was that I would make him do such a thing. But he did it. And I have to say, the Meccan is now a better man for it.

"Okay, okay," the Meccan confessed, flustered again. "It is this way. Everyone keeps saying it is 'this way' or 'that way' but nobody says where it is!"

My eyes glazed over and lost focus, as our next move wasn't clear. I was looking northwest toward the downtown area and then suddenly realized that I was viewing the exact place where the photo in my paper had been taken. "It's over there! Over there! The Valley of the Jews!"

Columb the Brit promptly cinched his leather belt a notch tighter and moved in the direction I was pointing. His legs took long, drawn-out strides that for a moment made our adventure seem like some Victorian foxhunt—and we had just spotted the bushy tail of our hidden prey.

Nobody was in the alley when we arrived. But out of the shadows a man in a uniform approached us with surprising urgency. He was private security. Paid to care.

"Salam," I greeted him, taking the high and respectful route. "We are journalists and have permission to enter. It is okay." I nudged the Meccan to make sure my bumbling Arabic was coming through. He smiled.

Of course it was not okay and we didn't have permission, but what the hell? It was worth a shot.

But the guard wasn't buying it. He radioed in his team, uniformed men in new Dodge Chargers with tightly groomed black moustaches (the mark of secular authority in any Arab country), and they came over. After a lot of bad noise, we settled on a deal: we had no more than two minutes to look at the wobbly synagogue, we couldn't go inside, and under no circumstances under the sun could we take a picture.

Seeing what else we could get out of the deal, we protested a bit, channeling Turkish bazaar etiquette, but that was it. And strangely, after all the assertiveness by the guards, they didn't even follow us up to the looted synagogue, as if they were actually freaked out about the Valley of the Jews or something . . .

"Okay, Columb, I'll do something crazy to create a distraction, and you start snapping pictures like some goddamn speedfreak paparazzo. Those swine think they can get in the way of subjects of the Queen and journalism, do they? What are they going to do about it? Hell, we've got the House of Lords to gripe to!"

Columb the Brit laughed long and hard on this bit, but we quickly swallowed the joke when one of the guards glowered at us from around the corner, as if we were visiting someone in prison.

"Okay, okay, Jesse," the Meccan said, trying to break it all up. "You've seen your Jew house. We should go now. They've got a job to do. You can come back when it's finished. Let's go."

He had a point. There wasn't really much to see, though the setting was cool: the magnificence of Hariri's mansion in the background, the downtown area, the blown-up buildings, and the site of the Rafiq Hariri assassination. A cozy little synagogue rested in the middle of all this conflict; it still somehow stood. At some point in the Lebanese Civil War, Amal militants had broken into it, destroying everything and spray-painting their thuggreen graffiti on the outside walls, as if to say, "Come and get us, motherfuckers!" Except, of course, that the tiny Lebanese Jewish community wasn't going to do anything about it—though their Israeli brethren were already busy blowing the goddamn bejeezus out of the country, making their own contribution to the polarization of Lebanon. So maybe nobody got the "upper hand."

Just as we were about to give in to the guards and leave, I brushed the Meccan's shoulder. "Hey, check it out!" Through the black rail fence and the wiry green vines, a beautifully blue, seven-candle menorah still rested atop one of the Roman-style arch windows.

Both Columb the Brit and I snapped a picture, disregarding the rules and willing to pay the consequences. It was amazing. Like a symbol of Hanukkah, and the actual outlasting of something. A sign that said that after everything, the Jewish people were still alive. It was unexpectedly powerful. I nearly choked up, actually.

MOHAMMAD AL-AMIN MOSQUE
· (BLUE MOSQUE)

Put your trust in Allah, but tie up your camel.

ISLAMIC SAYING FROM ARABIA

Not that it makes a bit of difference, but Jews are "people of the book" in the Koran and are considered a protected people. It made the Meccan very uncomfortable to look at the clunky old synagogue, which nearly every other set of eyes seemed to carelessly overlook. There was something about the taboo of it all, something in what he'd heard about Jews and Israel that just freaked him out.

That moment of looking at the ruined old synagogue, though ever so brief, was his first real-life encounter with Judaism. It's *not* like he went on a fourth-grade field trip to a Holocaust museum growing up in Saudi Arabia—rather, he grew up watching strict Arabian Salafist and Hezbollah TV. So just standing next to something Jewish was a big deal for him. It was something that he had to push himself to do, and it was uncomfortable for him.

It was no secret that he soon would be done with his bachelor's degree and would return to the public charities of Saudi Arabia, where a well-paying job and a fine Muslim girl to marry were all but inevitable.

Before he came to study at the Lebanese American University, life was pretty simple for the Meccan. So coming to Beirut, with all the cool and crazy things he was exposed to, was the most radical thing he'd ever done. It was his exploration of the world. Through his experiences, he expanded his consciousness and was really able to examine his individual and personal power. With the hope, of course, that the growth he gained in Lebanon would shine a positive light on the rest of his life. It already was.

———————

Just after leaving the Jew House and getting some food, the three of us killed a bit of time walking around the newly redone streets of downtown Beirut. There were flocks of people from different countries all around. I kept remembering back to when I was in Lebanon in 2007, on the same streets when nobody was around. Eventually, we came upon the very same mosque that Jeffery and Jimmy and I had once stood at with liquor in our veins—without a trace of the Hezbollah camp that had closed the Lebanese capital and brought Beirut to its knees. It was almost like it never happened. And feeling awed by it, I thought about telling the Meccan about our drunken stumble into the Hezbollah camp but decided not to. He had just asked Columb and me if we wanted to go inside the Blue Mosque with him.

Hell yeah! I thought.

But that's no frame of mind to be in when you enter a mosque. First, you need to clear your head of all silly things. Then you walk up to the entrance, take off your shoes, and enter solemnly—as if humor were a concept yet to be invented by humans. There was no need for it. Not for the Mohammad al-Amin Mosque, or Blue Mosque, in downtown Beirut. It is just that beautiful.

We walked together into the mosque.

Few people were in the mosque while we were there. We had arrived between the five daily prayers nominally observed by all Muslims. We went over to a far corner near the back and lowered ourselves onto the carpet, with repeated embroidery of a red Islamic arch. I leaned my head back, gazing in awe upon the complexities of the mesmerizing patterns in the diamond-shaped ceiling.

And then, the muezzin started his overture for the call to prayer. The two-minute warning was upon us. The Meccan turned, slowly, asking us if we'd wait for him inside while he prayed. Columb and I felt honored . . . and so did the Meccan. We had gone to the Jew House, where I did my quasi-religious thing—and now we were at a mosque, doing his religious thing. This was true education—and one of the best things I've ever done while waiting for a body of water to kick up waves.

GMAIL.COM

Weapons speak to the wise, but in general they need interpreters.

PINDAR, *Olympian Odes*

Somewhere between my rounds of "big beers" at the Duke of Wellington, I checked my email from some doggish, virus-infested Lebanese computer. No Microsoft Entourage, which I normally used on my computer. Which meant that Gmail chat popped up— something I had no idea even existed. And sure enough, there was dear old Lee, coming in at the bottom of the screen, hot on the wire, traveling by way of technology from Israel to Lebanon. Not going through the inland desert. *Instant communication!* Just no surfboard.

Lee: Dude, are you alive? Any waves? Have they cut off your penis?

Jesse: Leeeeee! You fucking hippie! Yes, to all . . . tho no more than the Jews did!

Lee: Ahahah! How big was it? The WAVES, I mean.

Jesse: Ha! Same as Haifa, man. Chest/shoulder high here. Same for you?

Lee: Yeah, about the same . . . same coastline, right?

Jesse: Oh, yeah!

Lee: So . . . you shoot any rockets yet, you bastard!?

Jesse: Jesus, man, no! Saw one driving thru south Beirut in
              the middle of the street a while ago as some sort of
              Hezbollah display . . . it was pointing SOUTH . . .
              can get crazy here, man. We also scored this place
              that apparently you guys blew in 2006. Oil refinery
              in Jiyeh. Remember?

Lee: Damn right!

Jesse: Easy! We don't know who else is reading this . . .

Lee: Yeah, wouldn't want anything bad to happen to you.
              BTW, I'd love to see Beirut. What's it like?

Jesse: Funny. Actually, kind of like Tel Aviv. A sister city
              . . . just replace the American-ness of Tel Aviv with
              a European vibe. More Frenchy, less hippie. No kib-
              butz Israeli chicks, either. High fashion rich . . . or
              just poor.

Lee: Ahh, well, not my thing. But nice. When I go out
              today I'll yell and see if you can hear me!!!

Jesse: Hahaha! OK, dude, tell your air force to take it fuck-
              ing easy this week. It's surf season!

Lee: Yes. Well, you tell Hezbollah the same.

Jesse: Yeah, well, it's not like I know them and go to their
              rallies or something . . . don't forget to yell next time
              you paddle out!!!!!!!!!!!

Maybe from the perspective of a virgin tight ass who lives a thousand miles from the Middle East, this chat is obscene. But that virgin lacks perspective. Everything we talked about was based on the 12,000-pound elephant of the Eastern Mediterranean: the inevitability of the next round of conflict. Everyone knows it's coming. And so we must remember that there is no peace. Just an absence of war.

SABRA AND SHATILA
REFUGEE CAMPS

We are all capable of carrying out acts of evil. That's the great lesson you learn as a war correspondent, and probably the most disturbing. That the line between the victim and the victimizer is razor thin. That in moments of fear and instability and social disintegration we all have the capacity to carry out acts of atrocity, or at best stand by as silent accomplices. And almost no one is immune. The contagion of the crowds sees to that. When you externalize evil, you turn human beings into extractions. Human beings like Muslims, for instance. That no longer grieve, or love, or suffer like we do. But embody a virus that must be eradicated.

CHRIS HEDGES

It was just after noon in West Beirut when my black-and-white Lebanese cell phone started to buzz. I was sitting under a big green tree on a brown park bench, enjoying a fine breeze and watching a bird, as my mind was still numb from studying Arabic all morning. I remember feeling a serene sense of coming out of something, introverted, and in a beautiful state of zombie-like Zen. I passively let the phone jiggle in my shorts a few more times. Then, I reached down to get it.

It was Yasmine, a friendly, 30-year-old Palestinian whose family had relocated to Puerto Rico from the days of the civil war. But I missed her call, and a text message mixing her three fluent languages of Spanish, Arabic, and English followed: "*Hola*, *habibi*, do you want to visit Sabra, Shatila?"

My jaw clenched as whatever peace had fogged my mind started rapidly to burn off, and I knew I'd be in for one of those profoundly disturbing experiences that I'd never want to forget.

———

The Sabra and Shatila camps are just south of Beirut and function as a temporary home to more than 12,000 Palestinian refugees. Since the UN set up the camps in 1949, six decades have gone by. Most of the people living in the camps were born as refugees, and it's the only life that they, and most likely their parents, have ever known. Out of the 59 officially designated refugee camps in Lebanon, Jordan, Syria, the West Bank, and the Gaza Strip, the camps in Lebanon are the least integrated into their host country. In 2007, Amnesty International denounced the appalling conditions suffered by over 400,000 refugees in Lebanon. But nothing changed.

Prior to the 1948 creation of the Israeli state, Palestinians lived in British-administered Palestine. Before that, it was Ottoman-controlled Palestine, where, since the Arabian invasion in the seventh century, the inhabitants were mostly Sunni Muslims and of Arab stock. But the reason for change was the mass immigration of Jewish Zionists—who came to create the state of Israel, and challenged the status quo. Land was both bought and seized, and many Palestinians fled. Settled Palestinian families didn't just leave their homes because the surf in Lebanon was so much better. It's always been the same coast.

The next push of Palestinians into Lebanon came during the Arafat era, or more specifically, the "era of regrettable events." Black September. When the PLO was expelled from Jordan and waves of Palestinians—both fighters and families—came on foot with whatever was on their backs.

It's easy to understand why all these Palestinian refugees made many of the Lebanese nervous. Especially the Christians. Nearly a fifth of the entire Lebanese population now consisted of mostly Sunni Palestinians, which threatened to throw off the entire power-sharing system by which Lebanon was governed. The Palestinian refugee camps, originally set up for the 1948 refugees, were hit with a new wave of Palestinians from Black September—not as anything planned, but as just a place to go for a people whose future was not yet clear. The Zionists didn't want them; neither did the Jordanians, and the Lebanese didn't want to deal with any of it. And so battles were fought, people died, and the Palestinians were mostly confined to their state-within-a-state camps . . . until something broke. And that, of course, was the PLO—when they (not the Palestinians themselves) were kicked out of Lebanon.

When the Phalangist militia stormed into Sabra and Shatila, the PLO leadership—including Yasser Arafat himself—had already fled to Tunisia. So the camps were open and unguarded and left to the onlooking Israelis and their Christian allies . . . they ravaged the place like Genghis Khan.

Today there are 12 Palestinian refugee camps in Lebanon. Some of them are open and resemble districts of larger urban slums, while others are closed, giving off a cattle-ranch vibe, as if they control dangerous beasts. They are designed to contain the unresolved Palestinian crisis—but they are designed to forget about it, too.

———

Seven of us piled into a minibus in West Beirut that day. Our connection was with Yasmine, who arranged the trip with a neatly-dressed Palestinian man who worked for an NGO in the camps. And as we drove away from the malls and shops and glitzy flair of Hariri's West Beirut, I got a feeling in the pit of my stomach that we were headed for the worst place in the world and we didn't even know it yet.

The Sabra and Shatila refugee camps were the battlegrounds of the bloodiest single event in the Arab-Israeli conflict to date.

The guilty were those of the Kata'ib Party—with their Nazi SS–inspired Phalangist militia. These were the Christian nationalists who couldn't stand what they saw as the Islamic takeover of the Lebanese state . . . which was violently highlighted on September 14, 1982, when the rising star of the Kata'ib Party, President-elect Bashir Gemayel, was assassinated. Fury was raging through Lebanon. And seeing an opportunity, Israeli defense minister Ariel Sharon helped arm the Phalangist militia with mostly American-made weapons and sent his men to watch as a not-so-meek band of crusading Christians committed a massacre that raised hell to earth.

Now, decades later, we approached the gutted remains of that conflict, in a post-traumatic gloom—only a few lazy miles south of Beirut along open the highway, about as far from the prospect of Jiyeh surf as emotionally possible. What lay in these camps was a savageness that proved atheism, nihilism, and the fucking animal in man.

As our van rolled down the same south Beirut highway that led to Jiyeh and eventually to the Israeli border, it broke hard near a massive stadium, which most tourists carelessly glance at as they pass between Beirut and the airport. And there I was, where I got my first glimpse: in all their chaos, the camps. Sitting as one, right next to each other: Sabra and Shatila.

As our minibus sped around a pothole-ridden rode along the perimeter of the camps, the neatly dressed Palestinian man from the NGO motioned for us to stop. We all shuffled out, making our way toward the de facto gate of the camps. Guarding it were a few Palestinian men in casual clothes, to whom our guide said a few words, and they let us pass. *Wasta.* That was key. It's Lebanese Arabic for "who you know," and apparently the PLO leadership, which nominally was in control of the camps, had approved our visit.

"Over here," the man called to our small group. But we were too stunned to move. We were frozen, taking in the haggard street, the ragged shops, the trash heaps, and the torn awnings. There was not a holy chance in hell that anyone had taken the time to think about any of it. No planning. There was no standard of infrastructure: no organized power grid, no main water system, and no sewage beyond what individuals made for themselves. Just a tangled mass of inhumanity. Worse than a Rio slum, this was an open-air prison—with the Lebanese Army, Syrian intelligence, Hezbollah, and other factions surrounding the place, keeping the Palestinians in their cage. It reeked of DO NOT ENTER.

It looked like a bombed-out apocalypse. Every structure in the camps was built incrementally, with different shades of poorly mixed concrete somehow holding it all together. Under a near psychedelic web of tangled power lines, unfinished rooms were stacked dangerously on top of one another. Water tanks and stray ladders, bags, wood, rope, pipes, antennas, and all the other stuff made the place feel permanently under construction.

On top of one of the buildings I saw the green Amal flag, which signified the house wasn't Sunni Palestinian but Shia Lebanese. Many of the residents of the Sabra camp are Shia refugees, pushed up from the southern parts of the country from some war with Israel. There were few other places in Lebanon that I saw Amal and Palestinian flags together, but everyone in Sabra and Shatila could agree on one harrowing thing: the Israelis had put them there, and the Lebanese kept them locked tight. The mood moved between livid rage and sickly grief.

Still near the entrance, I snapped out of my cerebrum and caught up to our group, which had made its way to two war-torn billboards of slain Palestinians from the September 16, 1982, massacre, hung literally on top of the mass grave that remained. Over 4,000 dead; maybe more.

Beneath the sign was a single mattress with a torn brown blanket tucked around it, for the caretaker to sleep on. This mass grave was the one open field in the camps, its grass fed by human flesh. Yasmine stood to the right, next to the man who had brought us here. He was explaining the story of the camp. While he spoke, an elderly Palestinian man came out and told of his friend's wife, who was savagely gang-raped by the Christian

Lebanese militia not too far from where we were standing. He was there to watch.

In a sort of ailing state, I made a few notes in my little black book. I asked Ryan, an Indian-British kid in our group, if he had any words for my camera. He looked over in my direction, but not at me. A glimmer of sunlight sparkled down his cheek, as a tear fell from his eye. Utter silence. Perhaps the sanest response to standing on top of a mass grave.

I looked up at the sun in anguish. I wanted to tear my teeth out. I wanted to sink into the grave. I didn't know what I wanted to do.

Feeling the intensity fully, I walked back onto the main street and saw two brown ragamuffins walking barefoot upon a steaming mound of oozing waste—not just rotting household goods but dangerous construction materials, toxic chemicals, broken glass. All things to be avoided in the civilized world. Clearly, the Palestinians hadn't planned on still being in the camps—certainly not for decades. The plan had been to temporarily set up shop in Lebanon and "liberate Palestine," not resettle in some shithole that the Lebanese themselves were too scared to visit. Investing in this place would take away from the prime directive: get Palestine back.

"Ahlan wa Sahlan," a soft voice muttered over my shoulder, as I watched the kids sift through the trash mound. It was a lone shopkeeper with a hunched back, selling DVDs. Not straying too far from the group, I followed him over to his rusted rack, held up by a broken wooden broom handle. When I reached out and opened one of the DVD cases, there wasn't anything inside. So we just smiled at each other. *Was I really here for DVDs?*

My stomach churned and I wanted to vomit. The man said something, but I couldn't understand. I couldn't understand anything about this place. My eyes brimmed with tears, as I thought about the torn mattress and the keeper who slept on the mass grave.

———

Staying close together, our group continued down the main drag of the Sabra section of the camp. Occasionally cars would pass with cargo cages on top, filled with half-broken parts. We wandered into a valley of more makeshift buildings, with no construction standards and no authority to demand them. Just everyone hijacking everything, at every opportunity—a raw state of nature. Pure Thomas Hobbes.

On the far side of the street was a green, blown-out car next to another trash heap. I saw a massive blackened splotch of carbon on a concrete wall, where a fire had once burned. It seemed to be the back of someone's house.

Above the charred blackness hung a poster of Samir Kuntar, the Druze terrorist who on April 22, 1979, loaded up a small inflatable boat from southern Lebanon and crossed the Israeli-Lebanese border to sneak onshore and kill an entire Israeli family, murdering the youngest child with his bare hands. I felt sick. In a twisted and tormented place. Here, growing up to be like Samir Kuntar was something to be?

In every direction, I could see propaganda. It was as if the people who had hung it were advertising their credentials for resisting the madness that had put them there. Another poster showed a red-checkered militant from the Popular Front for the Liberation of Palestine, with a seething Photoshop-enhanced gaze, clutching a holy Kalashnikov. Next to him were more posters: a young martyr in front of the Dome of the Rock in Jerusalem, a pile of Katyusha rockets, unknown bearded clerics, a militiaman in a black mask posing with guns in front of a flag. And so it was only a matter of time until my eyes wandered over to the poster of Saddam Hussein. A man who had made a few gestures to the Palestinian cause in his time, though not exactly a fucking humanitarian. But who cared? These people were locked in this camp, doomed to failure, and subject to a life of state-sponsored Lebanese apartheid.

Without doubt, the living conditions in Sabra and Shatila were the worst I've seen in the Middle East. Far worse than what I had seen in the West Bank. These camps were the untold catastrophes of the Israeli-Palestinian conflict. They were all but forgotten by the international community, largely overlooked by the Lebanese state. The camps were a place to bury issues that had all but lost hope of being resolved, while generations withered away.

Civilian populations are not terrorists. Caging them, not more than a stroll from the fine Lebanese sea I was once surfing, was an assault on humanity. Fuck it. Drop the bomb. To me, Sabra and Shatila were everything my Jewish ancestors learned to recognize, loathe, and stomp out from our species from their experience in czarist Russia. How could anyone bear to see anything similar happening here? Or anywhere?

The sun was dead-high, and the beat of chaos was still strong. We were off the main street, walking through a side corridor that swerved through the camp like a broken circuit cable. There was oxidized white paint on some of the concrete homes, but most had been left to the elements. Blackened mold, not from fire, but from humid rot, gave the place a stink known to all who have ventured into any Mediterranean slum. Running vertically down the walls were water and drainage pipes, loose wires, broken light sprockets, and torn propaganda, making the place look like a scene out of an old Soviet film. Everything was done at minimal cost and effort. A makeshift maze of random walls, like a deck of cards, waiting for one incoming shell to reduce the place to bloody rubble—if anyone ever bothered to waste a shell.

Still within the corridor, I noticed water trickling out of an overhanging second-story house. It was splashing all over the dirt of the narrow passage, forming a puddle, causing mud and near accidents when men on motorbikes occasionally came thundering past. Barely dangling out of the overarching concrete building, I could see a snipped hose that funneled the water—and I could hear a body shuffling around the wavering floor. This was a shower that pissed directly down on purpose! That Ryan kid and I could hardly believe it. It was dangling right over the alley!

Next there were the kids. Everywhere, there were kids. But these kids had firecrackers and kept shooting them off—one lighting, the other holding, and both yelling, as they teamed up, playing their favorite game: Palestinian guerrilla, where you pretended to launch a rocket and yell, "For you, Abu Ammar!" Abu Ammar was another name for Yasser Arafat.

Resistance was bred in the blood here. What else did they have? Playing Palestinian liberator made fine sense. Everywhere these kids turned were the markings of violent resistance and stories of the generations before, romanticizing about Palestine—*Home!* The most divine utopia to these people . . . but if they'd only known. The rural old Palestine that existed in their grandparents' stories was gone. Israel was there now. They didn't even have the slightest idea what it looked like. One of the most modern countries in the entire world—and yet, sleepy old Palestine was the dream they refused to wake up from.

Jesus, if they'd only known . . .

———

Abruptly, the Palestinian man who had taken us into the camp stopped for a moment, as if he had lost his way. Then he turned left at a fork, seemingly no different than any of the others in the narrowing corridor, and walked up to a green iron door and knocked. All eight of us huddled close. A woman in her 20s opened the door, dressed in a black coat and a headscarf with a pink flower design. She knew we were coming and welcomed us.

When we entered her house, I noticed that the exterior more or less resembled the interior: concrete blocks were stacked without any attempt to smooth a finished product or make things homey and warm. In a refugee camp, it's more comforting to make the place feel temporary.

She proceeded to walk us into a sort of living room, where the four corners were lined with old red couches. On the walls were cloths embroidered with Islamic calligraphy, pictures of children, fake flowers, and a few Middle East–style checkered boxes.

Seated on a chair was an old man. He wore worn sandals, brown slacks, and a short-sleeved shirt with an Islamic cap. This was the end of the line, all right. And I immediately understood that our wandering through the camp had been building to this very moment: a first-hand account of how these people got here. From Palestine.

Indeed, this was the narrative of his generation, and the old man made it very clear after his introduction that he did not want to be recognized as an *individual*. He was just a man, who shared the same basic life of nearly all the Palestinians his age who had found their way into Sabra and Shatila.

He motioned for us to all take a seat on his couches, stuffed together and sticky from the humid heat of the day. He took a deep breath and began with pious Arabic greetings, wishing, of course, that peace be upon us. Members of our group gave the traditional return greeting. But the man seemed unaffected. He was locked—hellishly sinking into the feelings of what was obviously the most defining experience of his life.

"September 16, 1982. We had the massacre in this camp, but we cannot speak only to that," he said, starting into a Marlon Brando stream of consciousness that unfolded at its own pace. "Between 1936 and 1948, I remember that radicalism took over in Palestine. The British made a wall in the north like today's wall with the West Bank. It was the beginning of it."

I looked around; everyone in our group was already deeply disturbed. We all wanted to bawl for this man. That fucking Ryan kid—whom I really didn't even know—kept holding his right arm with his left, bending his head back, and listening deeply, though loathing every second of it.

The old man told us his family was from a village near Acre, just a few miles north of Haifa. They were fishermen, he said. And then, abruptly, his face twitched and his words stopped. The room grew tense, then went dead silent. One moment passed into the next and my attention was drawn into the thick, mold-ridden air that had all of a sudden become impossible to breathe.

Resting on the table behind the man was a hatchet I had not seen, the kind of rusted thing that you'd find at an archeological dig, perhaps not too different from Tell Makor, the fictitious site just outside Haifa that James Michener wrote about in *The Source*.

The old man brought it forward for us to see.

"Jewish gangs showed up one day at my family's house outside of Akka," he said. He was holding the hatchet high, rotating it as he gazed upon both the flat hammer and the arching spike that made it unevenly heavy. "The Jewish gangs chased us from our home in Akka with these . . . and if they caught us, they hit us on the head with them."

The old man thrust down the spike of the hatchet, simulating a strike. Everybody's stomach turned. But perhaps mine most of all—I had just been to Haifa, surfing and hanging out with the grandchildren of those who had chased this man from his home.

Weary of it all, I closed my eyes in the old man's living room. Vivid images started running rapidly through my head of all the space that ran along the open Haifa hills and down to the sea. I knew what it took to clear out these Palestinians—only tens of miles up the coast—now hidden within the deep layers of the horrid refugee camps in Lebanon.

After surfing on both sides of the Israeli-Lebanese border, I was really starting to get a handle on this place. In Haifa, I had ridden the waves with Israelis whose adrenaline blazed at night from the rockets raining down near their homes. I had been gassed in the West Bank, had snuck into a Hezbollah rally, and had tracked down an old synagogue deep in the Lebanese capital. I had seen the Sabra and Shatila refugee camps, where nothing could have prepared me for the tragedies lurking around me. And somehow, on the inland route from Israel to Lebanon, I ended up sitting on that old man's couch.

Cold sweat dripped down my forehead. My vision glazed over—without focus. And somewhere inside me I knew that I had stared straight into the eyes of an old Mediterranean ghost who had altered my soul in a way that can never be forgotten.

EPILOGUE

My Arabic course ended a few weeks after my time in Sabra and Shatila, and my Lebanese visa expired a few days later. My next move was in the direction of Damascus, Syria (to stay at Yusuf's house), to write up the article for the *Surfer's Journal*.

But before that, I had looked at Che with a parting sadness. There was the sweet good-bye of one last surf, then I left him with Monner in the northern Lebanese city of Tripoli.

Nothing could have been more comforting than Monner's words about my lighthearted companion. "Jesse, it's not like I'm going to break him big-wave surfing or something. Che will be waiting for you the next time. In the same place you guys were going to begin." And according to Monner's email the other day, he's looking better than ever.

I'm going to close my black laptop now. The sun is growing heavy on the horizon here in Santa Barbara, California, and there might be enough magic out there to supply my nerves with one last lonesome surf before the darkness takes over. I'm not bound to the Middle East like I used to be. This whole surfing from Israel to Lebanon bit really ran a number on me. And there are no conclusions—only a commitment to stay open, empowering my mind to look beyond the divisions of a divided world.

From the Santa Barbara Hills
The Colonel
May 2011

Poem of the Sea

. . . Eastern Mediterranean, millions of years and tears before ten toes two arms and a cranium came to it, there were waves . . . they ran across not the biggest pooling of water on the planet but a fascinating one that would hold a mystical gravity for its dwellers so profound that they would die over it again and again . . . and no presence has been more constant there than *Waves*—nothing more poetic and seamless than a storm from the West, strengthened by winds and pushing out swell that peeled across the top of the sea, eagerly looking for a faraway reef to bond with . . . The Wave—no point is more magical than this . . . *Everything!* is the feeling, when paddling and crawling one's body into this energy that has forced this force to pounce upward and sideways and explode over your head, transcending its brilliance and ancient mirth that lurks along this shore upon your body . . . and so it is, was, and so it shall continue to be: a power and might so brilliant that it allowed a look into the modern-day toils of the region, a way through, a maritime hump that will continue to break—noticed or unnoticed—for all who wish to partake . . . a burst of juice, like a gleaming bolt of Greek-god thunder, still sitting there, waiting for the next time, whenever that glory may be . . .

I took this picture just after I caught my first few waves in Jiyeh. This completed my mission of surfing from Israel to Lebanon.